Famous Fortune Fights!

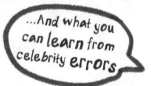

...And what you can learn from celebrity errors

By Andrew W. Mayoras & Danielle B. Mayoras

Legacy Expert Attorneys

Published by

Wise Circle books may be purchased for educational, business, or personal use. Books are available for special promotions and premiums. Please contact the publisher by email at trialandheirs@wisecircle.net or write to: Wise Circle Books, 278 Alamitos Avenue #2, Long Beach, CA, 90802.

FIRST WISE CIRCLE BOOKS AMERICAN EDITION PUBLISHED 2009.

Edited by DW Ferrell
Cover design by The Collectiv, Inc.
Interior design by Julie Keeler
Photography by David Studarus
Illustrations by Jo Dhammasvetakoon

The Library of Congress has catalogued the paperback edition as follows:
Mayoras, Andrew W.
    Trial & Heirs: Famous Fortune Fights! / Andrew W. Mayoras and Danielle B. Mayoras.—1st ed.
    p. cm.

    ISBN 978-0-615-32886-7
    1. Biographies—Rich People.   2. Law—Estate Planning.
I. Mayoras, Danielle B.   II. Title.

HT635.K4568 2009
288—dc22   2009939493

10   9   8   7   6   5   4   3   2   1

For our loving children,
AWM, BRM, and RSM, who light up
our lives and make us smile.

We love you.

table of CONTENTS
and STORIES

What's your story?

Learn how you can share
your own story on page 269

Section II

The Great Stork Derby

Do the words "living trust" scare you? They won't for long!
Trusts are the best tools to protect families from fighting over
money when someone dies. But, they have to be prepared and
used correctly to work for you.

Ray Charles
The Trust Kit Nightmare

A Lesson On "Trust"
Michael Jackson

The Wealthy Hedge Fund Manager Who Drowned
The Disinherited Child

The Jewish Clause
The Hard Working Plumber

The CEO Who Played Chess With Trusts

Section III

James Brown

Why do so many people fight over money after a loved one dies?
There are times when contesting a will or trust in court is well
worth it... and times when it isn't. We'll explore what lack of mental
competency and undue influence are — so you know your rights and,
more importantly, so you can protect your loved ones.

Section IV
ASSET DISPUTES – BUT THEY WANTED ME TO HAVE IT! 151

Danger! Danger! So many people take estate planning
shortcuts which only lead to regret. You'll find out why joint
assets, life insurance, and gifts can spark family fights that are
easy to avoid.

The "Official" Disclaimer!

As attorneys we can't pass up the opportunity to write a long-winded list of caveats in order to cover our rear-ends for every situation possible, in perpetuity, throughout the universe. First off, we are not affiliated with any of the celebrities and other individuals mentioned in this book directly. As legacy expert attorneys, we have researched directly with courts and primary sources and have diligently reported these stories to the best of our abilities. That said, each story has at least two sides to it, so we're quite certain someone somewhere will be a bit miffed we didn't tell it *their* way. ***Dear disgruntled alleged celebrity heir:*** We will gladly hear your side of the story, so long as you give us full rights to your life story, including movie and action figure rights. Deal? For those who read the advice in this book, and have unexpected problems, please understand that this book is intended to get you started in the process, and is not meant to be the encyclopedia of estate planning. Also, things can change. Today's tax advantages may be useless tomorrow and laws range widely from state to state. How widely do you ask? In Maryland it's illegal to take a lion to the movies, Illinois law won't let you fish in your pajamas (how unreasonable), and Californians can't set a mouse trap without a hunting license. No kidding! And for gosh sakes, please don't go out and think you know more than all of us attorneys by trying to create your estate plan yourself. Furthermore, by reading this you agree that James Brown is still the Godfather of Soul, Michael Jackson is still the late King of Pop, and Princess Diana should have been the Queen of England. Lastly, you promise to take this book and use its stories to start a conversation with your loved ones about estate planning. We hope you end up having the peace of mind we do, being assured that your legacy will pass on to your loved ones without mischief and hi-jinks to spoil an inheritance in probate court. Oh, wait! One last thing. You promise to buy a copy of this book for each member of your family, and sign up for updates at TrialAndHeirs.com. We know, shameless plug! But we want to get good information out there, and we need your help to do it. ;-) Finally, be sure to read the "fine print" when dealing with contracts, trusts, professionals, and smartypants like the authors who wrote this fine print.

Introduction

"Look, a fight!"

Who wouldn't look? Everyone loves to watch a good fight! As long as they're at a safe distance, right? And celebrities certainly make it more interesting to watch, what with all their mansions and mistresses — it's time to grab a front row seat. Lights... camera... action for fame, fortune and fights!

Did you know that two thirds of Americans don't have a will? As legacy expert attorneys we've seen it all, and right in our own backyards. Unfortunately there isn't enough information out there, and the same mistakes made in private repeat themselves in a public probate court. Even Andrew's grandparents fell prey to a... well, we'll get to that later. Famous people and famous cases are safe to watch from afar. But when fights include loved ones, it's horrible to watch, and that's one of the reasons we wrote this book. With famous cases as our guide, we'll walk through the simple and complex aspects of wills, trusts, estate planning and virtually everything you'll need to get you on the right track.

We hope you'll use this as a resource for family discussion and ensure that every adult in your family has considered how they'll pass along their assets. And for you, we hope to help you wrap your mind around something that can seem daunting: planning for YOUR heirs. You don't have to be Paris Hilton to be an heiress. If you have children and loved ones, they will be your heirs someday.

So how can you make sure your loved ones will enjoy a foolproof estate plan? This book will help your family avoid going to trial in probate court and avoid 'errors' as you plan for your 'heirs.'

What are heirs and beneficiaries?

An "heir" is someone legally entitled to inherit from someone who died. There are two ways to become an "heir." The first is when someone dies without a will or trust; then the family members become heirs under the law. The second is when someone dies with a valid will or trust. The people or entities (charities for example) named to inherit in the will or trust are called "beneficiaries." They are the ones who benefit.

Beneficiaries are also considered to be heirs. Someone who dies always has heirs (unless they have no family members at all). But someone who dies will only have "beneficiaries" if they do estate planning and name them.

Here are a few snapshots of real case stories and what we can learn from them:

Jimi Hendrix

The man whom many regard as the greatest guitarist ever known died in 1970 at age 27. Because Hendrix didn't have a will, his father received everything. He helped turn the modest estate into an $80 million dollar venture.

So what happened when Hendrix's father died? Hendrix's brother and half-sister waged a legal battle over the estate that lasted years and cost millions. When the dust settled, one was left out in the cold, with nothing. Who that person was may surprise you.

Learn why it is important for everyone to do estate planning to protect families from fighting, no matter how old they are... the consequences of waiting to take care of it "some day" can be devastating.

Frank Sinatra

Ol' Blue Eyes and his crafty estate planning lawyer helped pioneer

3

What is probate?

There's a reason "probate" rhymes with "hate." No one likes probate. It is the process through which the assets of someone who died are administered, through a court and overseen by a judge. It includes collecting the property and bank accounts, paying creditors, and eventually, distributing money to heirs. It can be a long, laborious and expensive process.

the concept of using a will to prevent a family battle over the estate. He used special language that made sure his wishes were respected.

But Sinatra didn't do everything right. He failed to follow basic planning steps which would have kept his final wishes private and his family away from probate court altogether.

Not all estate planning is the same. Having a will is a good start, but it's not enough for most people. Find out why. Discover how a trust is the better alternative.

The Great Stork Derby

A wealthy Canadian attorney died just before the Great Depression. Because he had no family — and had a mischievous nature — he created an unusual trust. He left most of his vast wealth to the woman (or women) in Toronto that gave birth to the most children during the ten years following his death.

This sparked many legal challenges and a great deal of debate. It also captivated a downtrodden nation that cheered on the many women battling for the prize… during a time when everyone searched desperately for hope.

Revocable living trusts are the best way to pass on legacies and protect families. You don't have to be afraid or intimidated by them. Learn, in plain and understandable English, what they are and how you can use them to safeguard your wishes, no matter how complicated or unusual they are.

Princess Diana

Even celebrities and the very wealthy who hire the best estate planning attorneys around can still make mistakes that open the door to expensive and public legal fights.

Lady Di left a detailed will to pass along her vast estate, naming her sister and mother as executors. But she also wrote a separate letter expressing wishes that were different than the will. So what did her sister and mother do with those wishes? Not what you may expect.

People who work with good lawyers to create wills, trusts and other estate planning documents are smart. But sometimes they later mess up everything they did right. Learn the pitfalls that can happen when you use joint bank accounts, add a name to the deed of your house, or take other steps to undermine your will or trust.

Martin Luther King, Jr. & Rosa Parks

For all the great things Martin Luther King, Jr. accomplished, he never took the time to make out a will. Rosa Parks did; she chose the people she most trusted to manage her legacy.

Yet both estates faced similar expensive and lengthy court battles. Why? Because the beneficiaries believed that the executors kept things secret and didn't properly manage the estates.

Even the best estate planning documents can't avoid legal feuds when those in charge fail to do what they are supposed to do. Beneficiaries and heirs have rights. Learn what they are and what executors and trustees should do to prevent legal challenges.

Anna Nicole Smith

Considered by many lawyers to be the Granddaddy of all estate feuds, the battle between the former Playboy Playmate and her "step-son" (who was 27 years older than she was) will seemingly go on forever. It has already gone through multiple trials, appeals, and challenges. It's even been to the United States Supreme Court.

And it all started when a 89-year old billionaire married a 26-year old stripper.

You'll learn from younger celebrities such as Heath Ledger, musicians such as Whitney Houston, politicians such as Edward "Ted" Kennedy, athletes such as Ted Williams, and national and international millionaires and billionaires.

Finally! An explanation for these celebrity debacles you've watched on the news! You'll have a front row seat in the courtroom while we replay the scenarios and point out what went wrong, the winners and losers, and what you can learn from it. You will even discover how to use these interesting stories to get parents and other loved ones to have the "dreaded conversation" about legal planning for death that can be so hard to discuss for many people.

These cases attest to the dangers posed by the lack of good legacy planning, but they don't just happen to the rich and famous. You'll also marvel at the trapped farmer who scratched his will into a tractor bumper, the richest woman in Asia who seemed to have left everything to her feng shui master, and a nurse who injected Viagra-like medicine into her elderly boyfriend to coerce him out of his money.

We have seen first hand how families can be torn in half when the legal planning is not in place or is not done properly. The combination of Andrew's expertise as a probate litigator and prolific blogger and Danielle's repute as an estate planner and captivating educator will help you delve deeper into stories you are already familiar with. Then you can learn what went wrong case by case and share how to prevent those mistakes in your own planning.

Will, trust, and other legacy contests are some of the most emotional, difficult, and expensive court cases that anyone can go through. Learn what rights you have if you are facing one, or if you are thinking about challenging a will or trust, attacking a gift or joint bank account, or questioning the actions of an executor. Better yet, learn everything your family can do to prevent these legal battles before it's too late. The best fight is one that never happens.

Poor estate planning can even affect families decades after someone dies, as we'll see in the details of Jimi Hendrix's story.

Are you ready to learn what you can do to avoid family fights — and what options you have if you're in one? And, of course, be entertained along the way? Read on!

Andrew & Danielle

the TRUE STORY
of JIMI HENDRIX'S LASTING LEGACY!

The man widely considered to be the greatest guitarist ever known left a legacy of brilliant music that was cut short by his tragic death at the age of 27 on September 18, 1970. Thirty-four years later, his remaining family members, along with reporters and fans, packed a Seattle courtroom to hear what would become of his financial legacy.

What is Intestate?

Intestate essentially means "without a will." So in the case of Jimi Hendrix, Jimi's estate was intestate. This means the laws of the state he lived in when he died determined who inherited his assets. Later you'll learn how this can affect a spouse, as with Sonny Bono's story.

Leon Hendrix was Jimi's brother, six years younger. Despite often living in separate foster homes throughout their troubled childhoods, the brothers were close growing up and beyond. Jimi even took Leon on tour with him.

However, because Jimi died "intestate," his entire estate was left to his father, Al Hendrix. Leon received nothing pursuant to New York's intestate laws.

While Jimi's estate was not large when he died, his musical legacy was used to create a managerial company called "Experience Hendrix." It eventually grew into a venture worth upwards of $80 million, mostly through licensing.

So what did Jimi's father do with it? Despite his seventh grade education, Al did not want to make the same mistake that Jimi did. He created a will in 1973 and then updated it several times. Al's estate planning grew more sophisticated with each change, evolving from the first simple will to a series of complex trusts, managerial businesses and family partnerships. Sounds smart, right? Throughout these varied plans, Leon remained as a prominent beneficiary, typically receiving around 24 percent.

But Al changed the will and trust again on April 16, 1997. For the first time, Al excluded Leon and Leon's children. Everything (except for one gold record) was left for other family members, with the biggest share going to Janie Hendrix, Al's adopted daughter through a later marriage.

Janie barely knew Jimi Hendrix. In fact, Janie had only met Jimi a couple of times and was just nine years old when Jimi died. Despite her lack of relationship with her famous half-brother, Al put his daughter Janie in control of Jimi's entire financial legacy.

Shortly after Al died in 2002, from a long illness, Leon sued. He claimed Janie had taken advantage of Al's lack of education, deteriorating condition, and reliance on her to write Leon out of the will and trust. For years, Janie had openly questioned whether Leon was even Al's legitimate son. Leon felt she purposely drove a wedge between him and his father. Leon also balked at the careless way she managed the estate, bothered by how she allowed Jimi's image to be sold on air fresheners, golf balls, cell phone covers and even incense.

Janie defended the lawsuit, claiming that Al was competent, made his own decisions, and was advised by sophisticated estate planning attorneys. These were his wishes, not hers, she argued. These attorneys even videotaped Al signing his last will and trust. Al clearly stated on the video that he knew that he was cutting Leon out completely. Janie argued that Al had grown tired of Leon's demands for money and refusal to hold a steady job and complete drug rehabilitation. Ouch!

In the summer of 2004, the case went to trial. It lasted for more than seven weeks and brought each side's legal fees into the several million-dollar range. Yes, this case dramatizes how the legal system can really benefit from a poorly prepared estate plan!

When the dust settled, the judge issued a detailed ruling against Leon on every claim he made. While the judge felt Janie had not properly managed the trust — and wasn't very credible — he firmly believed that Al knew what he was doing when he changed his will and trust.

Leon appealed to a higher court, and then appealed again to the highest one in the state. He lost each time and finally had to give up the quest in 2007.

Do you think this marked the end of Janie versus Leon Hendrix? Think again. Leon tried to lick his wounds from the lost case by going into business with a partner... the same man who bankrolled his failed lawsuit. They created "Hendrix Electric Vodka" and even promoted it by claiming "it's like drinking with Jimi. The drunker you get, the more you think you're with him." Touché?

Janie was not amused and sued, on behalf of the Experience Hendrix company, to stop the drink-distributing duo in 2007. Again, the pair fought in court. While Leon won the first round in trial court, Janie appealed and came away victorious. Leon finally gave up, and Hendrix Electric vodka was no more.

Now ask yourself: If Jimi Hendrix had left a will and specified what should go to his brother Leon and other loved ones, do you think any of this would have happened?

Avoid a family fight!

Family feuds in court over wills, trusts, estates and other inheritance disputes typically have two factors in common: they are expensive and emotional. Neither side can be happy with how expensive, difficult and emotionally-draining the Hendrix war became. Leon gained nothing through his lawsuit. Similarly, Janie Hendrix spent years of her life, and millions of dollars, battling Leon through multiple court proceedings. Family feuds like the one that plagued the Hendrix family highlight an important lesson: the only good legal battle is one that never happens. Every family should take great care to do the proper planning in order to avoid ending up the same way.

Millions of people participate in probate court proceedings and related cases every year. Many of those become contested (challenged), often in dramatic and unexpected ways. While most don't cost millions and take years to resolve, like the fight over Jimi Hendrix's legacy, they are extremely important to those involved and can be very emotionally and financially draining.

People experience common emotions when a loved one passes. They have sadness that the person is gone, comfort from their memories, occasional bitterness over chances missed, and, at times, relief that suffering has finally ended. Family members also have added stress. The complications that follow the death of a loved one can cause emotions to boil. When this happens — particularly in complicated family situations such as second marriages and siblings who do not get along — they often explode into full-blown family fights.

With this book, we will help you learn how to protect your family from facing the difficult tangles that come with probate law, as well as your legal rights if you do face them. Through our combined thirty years of legal experience helping families, primarily in the fields of estate planning, elder law, probate and litigation, we have dealt with these issues time and time again.

We want to educate families so less people will be caught in the midst of these feuds in the future. We'll also help you learn what to do when you suspect your rights are being trampled or when someone else is causing trouble. In other words, we want to help people sleep through the night again instead of worrying about what will happen when they, or their loved one, dies.

But, we must caution that this book is not a substitute for legal advice. Quite the contrary, we never advocate taking a "do it yourself" approach. This book will put you on the right path, but you'll need an experienced and qualified guide to complete the journey. The best way to protect your family and legacy is by working with a qualified estate planning attorney, or a lawyer who handles legal disputes like those discussed in this book. So how do you find a good attorney? Here are several tips to get you started:

1. Look for an "estate planning" or a "probate litigation" attorney.

2. Ask people you trust and respect for a referral to an attorney.

3. Many attorneys will offer a free initial consultation, so shop around a little.

4. Ask for references, how many years they've been in practice and where they got their degree. Then research them online.

5. Good online attorney referral networks are emerging. Sign up at TrialAndHeirs.com for the latest information.

While we wrote this book to help people, laws do vary from state to state, so no one should rely solely on the information contained in this book to address any of these important legal issues.

At the conclusion of this book, we'll give you more detailed tips on finding good counsel in your state. But first, you need to know what to listen for when talking to an attorney, which is one of our main purposes: to educate you.

Once educated, and once you've selected an attorney, you can do the proper estate planning to preserve your family and legacy. They should guide you and help you avoid problems that can arise when planning your legacy. So consider this book your map and the attorney your knowledgeable guide on the path toward a solid estate plan.

How does this "map" work?

1. We've divided <u>Trial & Heirs: Famous Fortune Fights!</u> into five separate sections, progressing from the planning involved with wills and trusts, to the different ways that fights occur: will and trust contests, asset disputes and administration problems.

2. Each section starts with a brief overview and an introductory TRUE STORY, followed by several chapters educating you and your family on important legal concepts. At the end of each chapter, we include a TRUE STORY (and sometimes two) to illustrate what we've taught you.

3. But what good are these stories without practical lessons to help you? We conclude the stories with tips to AVOID A FAMILY FIGHT to give you concrete advice so you can apply the stories to your own family.

4. At the end of each section, we've included IDEAS TO SPARK FAMILY DISCUSSION. These will give you specific and practical ways to approach your aging parents, spouse and other loved ones. You'll learn what questions to ask and what suggestions to make.

5. Please don't be scared when you see unfamiliar legal terms. We've included SIDEBARS throughout the book to help you. In the courtroom, a "sidebar" is when the judge and lawyers talk privately about something that isn't for the public or the jury to hear. But our SIDEBARS bring you into the conversation by translating lawyer talk into plain English. Don't feel like you have to memorize these new words. We have a GLOSSARY OF LEGAL TERMS at the end of the book to jog your memory.

And we promise not to bore you! That's what the celebrity stories are for... to entertain you while you learn.

We hope you'll use the famous case stories in this book as conversation starters. It's hard knowing how to have the "dreaded conversation." Facing one's mortality is never easy. Many refuse to think about it, much less do the proper estate planning to address it. So what do you do? How do you begin talking to someone who stubbornly refuses to discuss it?

Tell them about the stories you read. Let them see — in an interesting and non-invasive way — what can happen when they let their procrastination and fear of the unknown stop them from doing what they know, in their heart of hearts, they should be doing.

Along with the true celebrity stories, we've also included a few select cases from our law practice. While these stories are also true — and just as informative and entertaining as the others — we have changed the names and a few details to protect the identities of those involved. But they are still based on actual cases. And for the celebrity stories, we haven't changed a detail. We compiled them from information contained in public records, newspaper reports and other reputable sources.

We sincerely hope your family never finds itself in the midst of a battle like these cases. The best defense is a good offense, which means preparation. When you have a difficult family dynamic, such as an uncomfortable second marriage, heated sibling rivalry or elderly parent who may have been subject to undue influence, it's all the more important to be ready. In these cases, it's better to expect problems and plan accordingly.

Other times, the trouble arises in unexpected ways, as in the true story of a jazz musician whose legacy was built on a secret.

the TRUE STORY
of THE JAZZ MAN WHO WAS A WOMAN!

Whether they involve celebrities or regular people, the stories generated by this area of the law can be interesting. Take the case of Billy and Kitty Tipton. Billy Tipton was a jazz musician who died in 1989 when it was revealed, for the first time, that he was actually (drum roll please) a woman! That's right, he... er, uh... she had been masquerading as a man throughout her life. Apparently, women weren't always allowed to play in certain clubs, so "she" became a "he" and launched a jazz music career. She never looked back. She kept the secret from everyone, including her spouse and children, for more than 50 years. (Seriously, it's true).

But that didn't stop her from getting married to a woman — Kitty Kelly — who was a stripper, no less. Her stage name was "The Irish Venus." Kathleen "Kitty" Tipton was married to Billy Tipton for 18 years; together, they had three sons. They were adopted, of course. (Well, at least they thought they were adopted.) Then, she had remarried after Billy's death, which added "Oakes" to her growing list of names and pseudonyms. But to keep things simple, we'll call her "Kitty."

So where is the famous fortune fight in all this? When Kitty died in 2007, she didn't have a will. Her estate consisted of $300,000 from the sale of her house. As often happens without proper estate planning, a court battled followed.

It pitted 41 distant relatives (most of whom Kitty didn't even know) against her three sons. There even was a mysterious woman diagnosed with paranoid schizophrenia suspected of being a natural child of Kitty, even though she was only 11 years younger than Kitty.

To complicate the case further, the three sons had been feuding with each other since Billy passed in 1989. Apparently, after the big news of the gender secret was revealed when Billy died, the older two sons took it really hard and changed their names. While battling for their father's estate at the time, they accused Kitty of being an abusive mother and a liar. They didn't believe her story that she had never had sex with Billy or seen him (or her) naked… and therefore didn't know the big secret. (Can you believe that?)

The youngest son sided with Kitty at the time, defending his mother. When the dust settled from that battle, Kitty and the youngest son inherited what little was left in Billy's estate, and the older two sons received a dollar each.

So, of course, the three sons continued to fight after Kitty's death. They each hired attorneys, in addition to the attorney for the estate. The youngest, known as "Little Billy," claimed he was the biological son of Kitty and entitled to inherit everything. The judge ordered him to take a DNA test and he refused, claiming he already had a birth certificate. But how can a birth certificate be valid when the person listed as "father" was actually a woman?

Eventually, Little Billy submitted to the DNA test and it was shown he was not the biological son of Kitty. The mentally-ill sister referred to as the "mystery heir" was also found to be unrelated.

But that still left the big question open of whether the three sons could be heirs. The answer turned on a legal doctrine called *equitable adoption:* a recognition of informal adoption.

Because none of the three had been legally adopted, could the judge still treat them as adopted because it would be unfair to do otherwise? It's not like it was their fault that their father was really a woman. Think about how they must have felt when they learned the big secret after Billy's death in 1989.

The judge initially said he couldn't treat them as heirs because the laws of Washington didn't allow for equitable adoption. But, after holding a three-day trial, the judge changed his mind and decided that the boys should be treated as legitimate sons. They could inherit after all.

But what did they actually inherit? After all the fighting and paying off creditors, there couldn't have been much left of the $300,000 for the boys. They likely each pocketed less than $50,000. It's not cheap for estates and heirs alike to wage legal battles like this in court, especially with so many attorneys involved.

Of course, all this expensive feuding and fighting easily could have been avoided with even basic estate planning.

Have you done the proper planning for your heirs?

Avoid a family fight!

If Kitty had done a simple will naming the people as her beneficiaries — sons, daughter, legitimate or not — this fight wouldn't have been necessary. Because she neglected to plan, the three sons, who had already been through enough emotional turmoil, were forced into a vicious battle against each other and distant family members. This fight ate up much (and likely most) of their inheritance. What a legacy to leave the children! Two deceased mothers, no father, and now there's such a rift between the three brothers, will they ever even speak to one another again? Children deserve better. Billy and Kitty's story is dramatic, but even the simplest quarrels can erupt into vicious fights if there's no estate plan or a flawed one — we've seen it! Every parent and grandparent owes it to their heirs to learn how to do the proper planning and discover what problems and pitfalls need to be avoided. Every family can benefit by knowing how to discuss these issues, overcoming procrastination, and making sure that their family doesn't end up fighting in court like the heirs of Billy Tipton and Kathleen "Kitty" Tipton Oakes.

SECTION I

A WILL IS SIMPLE, RIGHT? NOT SO FAST!

As the saying goes, where there's a will, there's a way... a way to protect your finances and pass along your legacy. Whether your estate is worth millions or is meager, it's necessary to consider how a will could help you make a plan for your loved ones. But did you know that a will is a public document, and if your estate is not planned correctly, you may be setting your loved ones against each other in a public court? Scary thoughts, but don't be discouraged... you've found the right book.

Many people assume that a will is something they can take care of later, or they sign it and forget to update it when a child is born or other changes happen. Many celebrities have been in these situations and worse. Luckily, you can learn from their examples and protect your legacy for your loved ones.

In Chapter One, you'll learn the BASICS OF A WILL. Most adults don't have wills and aren't sure why they need them. But, in fact, they do! And, as you'll see from the will of Chief Justice Warren Burger, not all wills are created equal.

Chapter Two explores the STRENGTHS AND WEAKNESSES OF WILLS. See why Sonny Bono should have thought a little more about a will before his untimely demise. His wife Mary would have thanked him. A will would have saved her a lot of time, money and trouble. But wills are not perfect; you'll learn why.

IS THIS A WILL OR A NAPKIN? Even handwritten wills — in the right circumstance — can be valid. Chapter Three uses examples such as the famous Howard Hughes will fight and the equally interesting but less celebrated, "tractor bumper will" to show how diverse wills can be. While never a substitute for proper estate planning, a handwritten will is sometimes better than nothing.

Chapter Four dramatizes the necessity to UPDATE THAT WILL, even if you're young, as with the case of Heath Ledger. Life means change; wills should change too. You'll find out what happens when wills aren't updated and when you should consider updating yours.

And Chapter Five answers the question many of us face, "MY MOM LEFT A WILL, NOW WHAT?" In a public probate court, seemingly anything can happen. But procrastinating only makes it worse. As the story of Olympic champion Florence "Flo Jo" Griffith-Joyner warns us, we need to make sure we keep track of family wills… not just our own, but our parents' and other loved ones.'

And here's a new saying for you…

"Where there's NO will, there's NO way." No way to have a say in how your legacy will pass, that is. It's far better to be like Frank Sinatra. He not only controlled his legacy, he used his will to help manage disgruntled family members.

the TRUE STORY
of FRANK SINATRA!

A will is the most basic estate planning document used to pass assets to the next generation. One of the limitations of a will is that it's a public record (all wills become public). Anyone can read any will probated in any court in this country. For celebrities and the very wealthy, this often makes for an interesting read.

Frank Sinatra's will presents a classic example. Ol' Blue Eyes died on May 14, 1998, at the age of 82, from a heart attack. He left behind a vast array of property and assets that were estimated to be worth between $200 and $600 million. Much of this great wealth was placed into a trust (and therefore, kept out of the public eye).

Yet, despite being someone who went to great lengths to protect his privacy, Sinatra also left behind a very detailed 21-page will dated May 1, 1993. It included 15 specific bequests. To his wife, Barbara, he left $3.5 million, several houses, royalties from some of his music, household furnishings and two automobiles. He included $250,000 to his former wife, Nancy, $1 million to a trust for his grandchildren, $100,000 to Barbara's son, $600,000 to his three children (for starters), and hundreds of thousands of dollars in gifts to a few close friends.

His children (all of whom were from his first marriage with Nancy) also received shares of his personal property, including his sheet music, and interests in certain business ventures.

But what of one of the biggest assets — the rights to control (and profit from) his name and likeness? Sinatra had formed a company years ago to manage those rights. His daughter, Christina Sinatra, took over management of the company at least a year before he died. But Sinatra gave that company exclusively to his wife Barbara, through the will.

Reportedly, Sinatra was well aware of the bitterness that existed between Barbara and his three children. He was worried that his wishes could provoke a fight in probate court when he passed. So, with the help of an experienced estate planning attorney, Sinatra included a very detailed "No Contest clause" (also called "terror clause") in his will.

What are these "clauses" about?

"Clauses" is a fancy word that simply means a section of a will. The "terror clause" or "no contest clause" can be found in many wills. It states that anyone who challenges the will (or trust) forfeits his or her entire inheritance, or receives less. Laws about the validity of these clauses do vary, but they usually make a fight in court more difficult. In essence, it's "win or lose it all." Not an easy choice to make, is it?

This clause spelled out — at great length — how anyone who took adverse legal action would be completely disinherited from the will and trust alike. They would get absolutely nothing. The will then listed thirteen different legal actions that would invoke this clause, including challenging the validity of the will, claiming entitlement to any asset through an agreement or promise, filing a claim (valid or invalid) for money against the estate, or even seeking (unsuccessfully) to remove an estate administrator.

This clause apparently worked. No one challenged Sinatra's will or trust in court. His wishes were respected, like it or not. While this clause may have disappointed his three children, it seems to have saved them and his wife alike from a very public, expensive and emotional battle.

Even in death, no one wanted to mess with Ol' Blue Eyes!

Are you worried your family will fight over your property when you're gone?

Basics of
a will

Chapter One

No one likes to think about his or her own mortality... and it's not easy to plan for. It's easy to procrastinate on issues related to "death" when you're busy "living!" The 'D' word isn't really a popular topic of discussion around the dinner table. But you know you need a will, and you owe it to your family to have one. But why is it so important?

Everyone knows what a will is, right?

Everyone does need a will. It is the starting point of every estate plan. And to begin estate planning, you need to understand what a will really is and what it can and cannot do.

A will is a legal document containing the directives of the "testator" about how to pass on his or her property after death. If a person dies with a will that is accepted by the probate court, he or she has a "testate" estate.

At its most basic level, a will is your message to your local probate court about how and to whom you want your property left, and what person you wish to administer it. And more importantly, if you have minor children, your will is the way to tell the court who you want to take care of your children if you unexpectedly pass on. Morbid thoughts! But what would happen to your

What's a Testator?

It sounds like "test-taker," but it's simpler than that: A testator is the person making the will. What's a "testate estate?" Simply put, it's the estate of the person who made the will. "Testate" essentially means "with a valid will."

children if you unexpectedly passed and didn't leave instructions for their care?

Indeed, wills are especially important for parents with minor children. A will is the place where parents name a guardian to care for their more precious commodities in case the unexpected happens. If the parents die without a will that names a guardian, the court will decide who gets to raise the children. This can set the stage for a difficult fight between relatives if your wishes haven't been made clear in a will.

A will is certainly not the most sophisticated form of estate planning, as Chief Justice Warren Burger's will dramatizes. But a valid one does achieve the primary goals of making sure your wishes are followed and your property is left as you desire.

Are you worried that a will is expensive? They're usually not. Because wills are relatively simple documents, the costs are modest and definitely worth it. Of course, many people have wills that cost them nothing at all. This is not without risk, but a homemade will is usually better than nothing.

the TRUE STORY
of CHIEF JUSTICE WARREN BURGER!

A will can be very simple, sometimes too simple. Consider the Honorable Warren Burger. He was Chief Justice of the United States Supreme Court, the most powerful judicial position in this country. The Supreme Court issues decisions that shape our nation and affect the rights of everyone in it. The Chief Justice has more say in these decisions than anyone.

Naturally, you'd assume that the Honorable Warren Burger would have created the most comprehensive estate plan known to mankind. Unfortunately, when Burger died, his family was left with a will that contained all of 176 words. That's it — for an estate worth more than $1.8 million. If you do the math, it comes out to $10,000 per word!

Too bad he didn't use a few more words. The family of the late Chief Justice was forced to spend thousands of dollars extra in probate court that could easily have been avoided if he had included certain language that is commonly used by all good estate planning attorneys.

Burger's will failed to give his co-executors (his son and an appellate court judge he trusted) the power they needed to sell real estate, pay taxes and otherwise manage the estate.

Accordingly, Burger's co-executors had to spend extra time (and money)

What is an executor?

Don't confuse this word with "executioner." Instead, think of it this way... an "executor" executes the will, and in a sense, they're an executive. The executor or co-executors administer the estate and make sure the wishes of the person who died are followed. Different states have different names for this legal position, including "personal representative" and "administrator." But for our purposes, they mean the same thing.

Basics of a Will

in court seeking the authority of the probate court to approve their actions. The really surprising part is that his will treated his two children unequally. He left his son two-thirds of his estate and his daughter only one-third. The meager will was ripe with opportunity for a fight between siblings.

Despite the flaws and the brevity, it was still a valid will. He included the important language that demonstrated his intent for the document to serve as his last will and testament. It accomplished the two main objectives: it disposed of his property and it named an executor to do it. Luckily, there were no minor children to worry about or he may have needed a few more words.

The will did not keep his affairs private, did not save legal fees or probate costs, and wasted hundreds of thousands of dollars on estate taxes that easily could have been avoided. But in the end, 176 words were all it took to pass on his $1.8 million.

Do you have a will yet?

Avoid a family fight!

A "homemade" will is usually better than not having a will at all, but what if something important is missing? Chief Justice Burger of all people should have known the value of a good lawyer. By not using an estate planning attorney to prepare a proper will — which likely would have cost no more than a few hundred dollars — Burger's heirs spent thousands. And worse, by leaving unequal distributions to his two children (his son received twice as much as his daughter), he should have been extra careful to do the proper estate planning. It is especially important to go the extra mile when dividing assets unequally to help avoid a fight in probate court.

Strengths and
weaknesses
of wills

Chapter Two

Strengths of Wills

A will is important because it ensures that the probate court knows what your wishes are. But do you really need one? What happens when you don't have a will?

In a way, there is a substitute will waiting for you. Every state has "intestate" laws that instruct probate courts how to dispose of property when someone dies without a will. Remember these from the Jimi Hendrix story?

Don't agree with how the state would decide what to do with your property? Tough. Do you even know what you state's laws say? No? Too bad. If you didn't leave a will, your heirs have no choice. An estate without a valid will is always considered to be intestate and defaults to laws that loved ones you leave behind may not agree with.

But is it so bad not having a will? Think your spouse would get everything? Unfortunately (for some) this is not the case. In most states, the spouse gets a percentage of the estate, with the rest passing on to the kids. The percentage varies from state to state. And what about the grandkids? They get nothing. In most states grandchildren only receive something under intestate law if their parent dies before the grandparent.

And who will fill the all-important role of executor to administer the estate? The judge will pick someone if you don't have a will. And if you have several children who can't agree on who should serve as executor, there may be a nasty fight! Sometimes, the judge might even pick an attorney or other outsider to administer the estate for your family.

For those with only a modest estate, and little concerns of a family dispute, a will may be all you need. In fact, even the most sophisticated estate plans still use wills. They work as a safety net to make sure that your wishes are followed, rather than the plan created by the state. Every good attorney who prepares a living trust also includes a will to make sure the trust does its job.

Weaknesses of Wills

But wills are far from perfect. Every will filed in this country is a public document that anyone can see. Anyone!

Do you like hearing about the private details of celebrities? Of course! Even a simple Internet search will lead you to dozens of famous wills, such as Michael Jackson, Elvis Presley, Paul Newman, Jacqueline Kennedy Onassis, Marilyn Monroe, Princess Diana and William Shakespeare, just to name a few. Your will would be just as public.

Why? Wills pass through probate court. Like most court documents, this means that they're public records. Would you really want a stranger or, even worse, a nosy neighbor reading your will and discovering how much money you had and to whom you gave it?

Probate court also leads to legal fees and other expenses, such as inventory fees, court filing charges, bonding company costs, payments to appraisers and more. Some estimates place the annual legal fees and costs generated from U.S. probate courts at more than $1.5 billion.

And as you know, if you've been through the court system before, nothing moves quickly in the courts. Sometimes wills are tied up in probate court for years. We've even seen cases of estates lasting ten years or more!

There is yet another concern. When a will is admitted to probate, the spouse, children and certain other family members of the decedent are entitled to receive a written notice, even if they are not beneficiaries of the will. Sounds like an invitation to cause trouble, right? It often is, unfortunately.

Creditors of the person who passed also must be notified. Anyone who is owed money (and sometimes, even those who aren't) will come rushing to probate court, hand extended, to collect from the assets of the decedent. Often the creditors can drain an estate before family members receive their share.

There are other limitations to wills as well. But do not fear — there is a better way. You'll learn all about it in the next section.

What is a Decedent?

It sounds like the combination of "deceased" and "defendant," but this word simply refers to the family member who has passed on. If it's your will that is being discussed in a probate court, you would be the decedent (and you'd be dead!)

Despite their pitfalls, wills are essential, a necessary foundation on which to build a solid estate plan. It's hard to imagine anyone who would prefer to leave the destiny of their legacy up to the intestate laws of the state. Yet for some reason, most people in the U.S. do not have wills. According to a study done by Consumer Reports, about two-thirds of all Americans do not have wills. The list of famous people who died without valid wills is long: Ulysses S. Grant, Jimi Hendrix, Buddy Holly, Martin Luther King, Jr., Abraham Lincoln, Karl Marx, Pablo Picasso and many others.

Estates without wills are almost always more difficult, complicated and expensive than those with one. And if you pass away without a will, your wishes will not be followed. Think it'll be okay if you tell people what you want done with your property? Unfortunately, that won't work. The intestate laws of your state — not your unwritten wishes — will still dictate what happens, even if everyone knows what your wishes were. And if you never make your wishes known through a valid will, you will never know who may come out of the woodwork.

the TRUE STORY
of SONNY BONO!

Sonny Bono (born as Salvatore Phillip Bono) never had trouble achieving success. His career as an entertainer was well known, but he didn't stop there. In 1988, Sonny Bono ran for mayor in Palm Springs, California and was elected by the widest margin in the history of the state. He then ran for Congress in 1994 and won too. It seemed like everything Sonny Bono tried, at least professionally, he accomplished.

It all ended with a dreadful skiing accident in Nevada. He died on January 5, 1998. His third wife, Mary Bono, was left to pick up the pieces. She hired an attorney and filed for probate in California. There was only one problem — Sonny had no will.

Mary applied to be executor over his estate. She listed the value of property in his name alone to be $1.7 million. Mary Bono also was forced to file special court petitions seeking authority to manage the significant royalties that were due.

Mary and her lawyer informed the court of unique and valuable business opportunities that were in danger of being lost. Because there was no named executor, no one had legal authority to make these decisions without a court hearing.

Mary should have been allowed time

What is a petition?

A petition is a legal document that lawyers file in probate court asking the judge to do something, such as approve a will, name an executor of the estate, or grant special permission to do something. In some estates — especially where good estate planning wasn't done ahead of time — it takes many, many petitions to administer the estate. In others, it may only take two (one to open the estate, and one to close it). Usually, more petitions filed in court mean more legal fees that the estate has to pay.

to grieve. Instead, she was dealing with the probate court while working out mortuary details, handling press inquiries, fighting off paparazzi, and parenting two minor children. Can you imagine the stress? Because there was no will or other proper estate planning, she had to hire an attorney and spend her valuable time — not to mention money — filing extra petitions in court to seek this authority which Sonny easily could have given her with a will.

Unfortunately, it went from difficult to worse. Mary also had to contend with claims filed by creditors of the estate, including one filed by Sonny's second wife, Cher, who believed she was still owed money from her divorce.

And Mary had one more problem to occupy her time. When she filed to open the probate estate, Mary dutifully listed Sonny's four children, including his two from prior marriages. But there was one child who was not listed; at least he claimed he was a child.

On July 2, 1998, a man named Sean Machu filed a legal claim and said he was the illegitimate son of Sonny Bono, born April 10, 1964. Reportedly, Machu's birth certificate lists Sonny Bono as the father, and Sonny admitted having an affair with a woman named Mimi (the name of Machu's mother) in his autobiography. He even paid her a cash settlement, but paternity was never established.

Machu, a struggling actor, hired an attorney to stake his claim. Mary's attorney objected to his request.

To resolve the problem, the judge ordered DNA testing to determine paternity. To do this, a blood sample had to be taken from Sonny Bono's body. The results of the blood testing were sealed. But afterwards, Machu withdrew his claim, as confirmed by his attorney. No one outside the case knows what the results were. Because of the secrecy, it is entirely possible that Machu was Bono's son and his claim was resolved through a quiet settlement... or maybe he wasn't Bono's son.

Either way, by the time the whole matter was sorted out, Mary

Bono had already successfully ran for her late husband's seat in Congress and turned her attention toward positive things. But for the better part of one year, she was forced to deal with this man claiming to be a son — obviously hoping to find his pot of gold — along with a host of other unnecessary problems.

Had there been a valid will — or better yet, more thorough estate planning documents — these headaches could easily have been avoided. If Sonny Bono had created a will that mentioned Machu and specifically included or excluded him, then paternity tests would not have mattered. Mary Bono could have easily administered the estate, and Sonny Bono's assets would have passed pursuant to his wishes, not the intestate laws of the State of California.

Have you asked your loved ones if they have wills?

Avoid a family fight!

There is no reason that two out of every three Americans should be without a will. Obviously, this group includes many people who should know better, and whose families have a lot to lose if there is no will. The added expense, aggravation, and time spent addressing problems and going to court can easily be avoided. And intestate estates are often magnets for trouble. Who will be the executor? Who gets what property? How are creditors to be dealt with? What decisions need to be made to protect the heirs? These are all questions that can be addressed through a will. Without a will, a judge must decide them. When families don't agree, it leads to infighting and conflict. Everyone owes it to their loved ones to prepare a basic will.

Is this a will or a napkin?

Chapter Three:

As Chief Justice Burger demonstrated, a document does not have to be fancy to qualify as a will. In fact, Honorable Burger typed his own will (and even misspelled a word). Other people handwrite their wills; these are known as "holographic" wills.

What are holographic wills?

A "holographic" will is one handwritten by the testator. When most people have wills prepared, they are done by an attorney and formally prepared on a computer. But handwritten ones can work too. The person writing one must clearly state it is intended to be a will, replacing all prior ones, and must sign it. Different states have other requirements as well.

In about half the states, holographic wills are accepted to probate even if no one signed them as witnesses (which is normally a requirement for wills). Additionally, in some states which do not recognize un-witnessed holographic wills, courts can still accept them in certain circumstances, as with members of the armed services on active duty, or if they were originally written in a state that allowed them.

The states which require all holographic wills to be signed by witnesses have a good reason for that legal requirement. When a handwritten document without witnesses is offered for probate, the first questions asked are: Was it really signed by the person who died? And if so, did he or she truly intend it to be a will? Witnesses play an important role to safeguard against these concerns. States that require witnesses are worried about forgery, lack of competence, and questions about what the signer really intended.

Other states have more relaxed laws about holographic wills. They would rather allow something to pass as a will than nothing. In these states, handwritten wills can even be accepted as valid if they are only scribble on paper. The intent must be clear and it must be handwritten and signed. It must indicate how the decedent wants his or her property to pass, and it certainly helps to name an executor of the estate (otherwise the court will decide).

That's all it really takes. In fact, it can work even for things other than paper. But even in these states, the question of whether the will was actually signed by the deceased person always remains subject to close scrutiny.

Handwritten wills are usually more suspect than wills done with a proper attorney. Sometimes, when holographic wills appear it only means one thing... a fight!

the TRUE STORY
of HOWARD HUGHES!

The scene: U.S. Highway 95, some 150 miles north of Las Vegas. The time: 11 p.m., December 1967.

The central character: Melvin Drummar, age 22, who drove from his job at a mine in Nevada to search for his wife who had run off with another man.

The discovery: One very scraggly man. Drummar said he found a filthy, unshaven man lying in the dirt.

The man needed help and a ride to Las Vegas. Not knowing who he was, Drummar drove him there and gave him some pocket change because the man had no money. Only then did Drummar learn the identity of his famous passenger. According to Drummar, it was Howard Hughes, the richest man alive at the time.

Howard Hughes died on April 5, 1976. Initially probate documents were filed in court stating that he died without a will. The Hughes Estate was determined to be intestate until a three-page handwritten document, dubbed by the media as the "Mormon Will," mysteriously surfaced on the desk of an official at a church in Salt Lake City, Utah. But who put it there?

This handwritten will bore the name of Howard R. Hughes and was dated March 19, 1968. Howard Hughes' distant relatives — cousins and uncles well removed — were the only heirs of his $2.5 billion estate if no will existed. So the heirs quickly challenged the document as a forgery.

Melvin Drummar swore otherwise. As well he should... he was left a 1/16th share (worth a cool $156 million) if the will was upheld. The case went to trial in 1978 before a Las Vegas jury. Well paid forgery experts testified for both sides. To no one's surprise, they disagreed over the will's validity. In the end, the jury did not believe Drummar's experts.

Or perhaps, they never did believe Drummar himself. He had a prior arrest for a forged check and steadfastly claimed he had never seen the Mormon Will. That is, he held to the story until his fingerprint was found on the envelope that contained the will. He then said that someone had delivered the will to him. Not knowing what to do with it, he slipped it into the church because it too was a named beneficiary in the will. Sadly for him, this story did not convince a jury of his peers. (Given his checkered past, and the fact he lied about finding the will, this probably didn't surprise many people).

Decades later, Drummar still swore the will and his story were legitimate. In fact, almost 30 years after the jury ruled against him, he filed a new lawsuit in federal court. With the help of a retired FBI agent who found new evidence to support him, Drummar claimed that he never received a fair trial. The judge ruled in 2007 that Drummar already had his day in court and the case had been "fully and fairly litigated" back in 1978.

Whether or not Drummar told the truth, one thing is clear — the richest man alive could have easily prevented this drama with a proper will, prepared by an attorney. That way, there would have been no question about Hughes' true wishes. Of course, given Hughes' well known eccentricities, perhaps this result was exactly what he wanted. *Have you taken a shortcut with your estate planning?*

Avoid a family fight!

Creating nothing but a handwritten will — especially one without witnesses — is a recipe for litigation. Even if your state accepts this type of will, no one can be certain if the document is legitimate, or if you were competent when it was written. This is especially true for someone who can afford an attorney and knows enough to hire one. People like Howard Hughes are used to working with lawyers, and he certainly had money to spare. There is no reason to rely on this type of shortcut when it is so easy to prepare a will the right way.

the TRUE STORY
of THE DESPERATE FARMER!

While holographic wills can create major problems, as they did in the Howard Hughes Estate, they can also be useful in the right circumstances. Such was the case for an unlucky farmer in 1948.

It was high noon on the 8th of June. Cecil George Harris of Saskatchewan, Canada told his wife not to expect him home until ten that evening. He latched his farming equipment on the rear of his tractor and rode out for the day. One hour later, Harris stopped to oil and adjust the tractor. When he climbed down from his seat, Harris accidentally shifted the gear into reverse. His tractor slammed into his body and pinned his legs. Harris's arms were unrestrained but he could not reach the gear to free himself. He was trapped.

When Mr. Harris did not return home by ten, Mrs. Harris became worried and went to look for him. He was conscious when she found him and ran to the neighbors for help. They soon freed Harris. He was rushed to the hospital still awake but Harris did not recover. He died less than two days later.

Harris's wife and two young children were left unprotected because Harris did not have a will. Or at least, that's what everyone thought. Not long after his passing, one of the neighbors inspected the tractor and noticed that the bumper had been scratched. These were not ordinary scratches that one would expect to find on a tractor bumper... rather these scratches contained the following writing: "In case I die in this mess, I leave all to the wife. Cecil Geo. Harris."

Another neighbor had discovered a knife in the pocket of Harris's clothes. The knife and the fender were taken to a solicitor (which is what some attorneys were called then in Canada).

The solicitor was able to make a copy of the writing and presented it and the knife to the local probate court. It caused quite a stir. The judge could locate only one case to provide legal precedence — a 1926 case from England in which a holographic will written on an eggshell was rejected because holographic wills were not valid there. Luckily for Harris's widow, the province of Saskatchewan — unlike England in 1926 — did allow holographic wills.

Many witnesses gave sworn statements for the court to verify that Harris really did intend the writing to serve as his will. A local banker testified that the signature on the bumper matched those on file at the bank. A doctor attested to the fact that Harris was conscious when brought to the hospital. The neighbors who found Harris verified his arms were free, and those who found the bumper and knife also signed sworn affidavits.

The probate judge was convinced. He accepted the bumper as Harris's holographic last will and testament.

But an original will must be filed when it is available. Accordingly, the judge ordered the section of the fender bearing the writing to be cut and filed with the court. This, of course, raises the question: How did that fender fit into the court's file?

Eventually, the fender found its way to the law library of the University of Saskatchewan, where it still rests today. It serves as evidence to all that the old adage certainly is true: where there's a will, there's a way.

Are your affairs in order in case an accident happens to you?

Avoid a family fight!

Don't wait for an emergency. If you don't have a will, write one now, and sign and date it in front of two people who are not beneficiaries under your will. Clearly indicate that it is your intent that the writing serve as your last will and testament and that all prior wills are revoked. Write directly and legibly and instruct how you want your property to pass. Name the person whom you want to serve as executor. It is always helpful to name at least one backup executor too. If you have minor children, name multiple guardians, in order of preference, to care for them if you and the other parent pass. Have the two witnesses sign your holographic will.

This method can only serve as a band-aid. Do not use this as a substitute for a proper estate plan (will, trust or otherwise) developed through a good attorney. And certainly do not rely on a handwritten document without witnesses. But by following this quick approach, at least your wishes should be honored if the unexpected happens before you can complete the proper planning.

Chapter Four

Have you been reading this Chapter and patting yourself on the back because you already have a will? Well good, that's a start. But go look at your will. How old is it? Is it recent?

Most wills have these words at the very top: "Last Will and Testament." Does this mean that once you sign a "last" will, you don't have to worry anymore? No! A "Last Will and Testament" is only the last will until you sign a new one. No will should be intended to remain in effect forever.

Why not? Life means change. New children are born. Even better (according to some), so are grandchildren. Sadly, some children die. New marriages happen, as do divorces. Think a divorce automatically cuts your ex-spouse out of your will? Not so fast. Laws vary about that from state to state, and what the divorce judgment says is usually the key. Don't take a chance. Even the best (or worst) relationships change, and people do as well. People's property changes too. A will created when you had a small home and even smaller bank account may make no sense at all as you advance in life and achieve financial success.

The general rule is that a will can always be changed as long as the person who signed it is still competent. There are a couple exceptions, such as when a husband and wife have created a "contract to make a will," meaning they both agreed to leave their property a certain way and never change it. But for the large majority of wills out there, change is not only allowed but is expected.

How do you change a will? There are two ways. One is to create a new will. But be careful, your new will must clearly state that it revokes all prior wills, or it will lead to confusion and possible conflict. The second way is to keep your will in place, but tweak it a little (or not so little). This is called a "codicil."

What is a codicil?

"Codicil" is a fancy word meaning amendment to a will. Sometimes, people do not need to redo their wills entirely. When only a change or two is needed, a codicil may be all they need. Not sure when you need a codicil or an entirely new will? When in doubt, ask a good estate planning lawyer.

When might you want to sign a codicil rather than a new will? For example, if you had two children and then are lucky enough for a third but everything else remained the same in your life, you may want to create a codicil to your will that adds your latest bundle of joy but leaves everything else the same. If you have more substantial changes, such as a divorce or a new plan for distribution, you are probably better served with a new will altogether.

When you do create a new will, you will be smart to destroy the old one. In fact, once someone physically destroys a will, it is considered "revoked" and invalid. For this reason, many good estate planning attorneys have their clients sign only one will and they do not keep a signed copy. That way, if the client ever decides to revoke the will, he or she only has one document to destroy.

Does this worry you about the possibility of accidental destruction? Maybe your three-year-old daughter decides to make confetti out of your will. Or your dog decides to relieve himself on just the right spot where you happened to leave it. Don't worry, while these certainly aren't ideal situations, a copy of a will — even an unsigned one — can often be admitted to probate when there is an accidental destruction or the original cannot be located. Of course, you certainly don't want your family confused over whether the destruction was accidental or intentional. Be safe. Keep your will in a safety deposit box or other secure location and out of the hands of your three-year old daughter.

Additionally, it is never advisable to destroy your old will without signing a new one immediately. Otherwise, you will be at risk for dying intestate during the time in between the destruction of the old and execution of the new one. Remember, intending to sign a new will is not enough — you must actually sign it for it to work.

How often do you need a new will? The standard rule of thumb that most estate planning attorneys follow is three to five years. Every three to five years, you should read your will, see what changes are needed, and in the case of more sophisticated estate plans, have it reviewed by an attorney. Why? Laws change; even laws about wills. Having a regular legal review of your will and other estate planning documents will make sure that any new changes in the law won't leave you with unintended consequences.

But the most important time to change your will is when someone you would plan to leave your property to dies or is born, if you experience a marriage or divorce or start a new business. You never want to take a chance on leaving your family unprotected.

the TRUE STORY
of HEATH LEDGER!

Heath Ledger was one of the most beloved young actors in Hollywood until his tragic death on January 22, 2008 at the young age of 28. Reportedly, his death was caused by an accidental overdose of prescription medicines. Heath was the successful lead actor in several popular films and certainly enjoyed a substantial fortune before his early demise.

Heath Ledger's will was written three years before he passed prior to his relationship with girlfriend Michelle Williams. More importantly, it was before the birth of their daughter, Matilda Rose, who was only two years old at the time of Heath's death. Heath's will left everything to his parents and sisters.

A matter of weeks after he passed, Heath's uncles, Mike and Haydn Ledger, publicly accused Heath's father, Kim Ledger, of mismanaging their grandfather's $2.5 million estate. They raised fears that Kim would not properly care for the interests of Heath's daughter. They encouraged Michelle William's father, Larry Williams, to hire an attorney for the family to protect Matilda's interests.

Days later, it was revealed that Heath's father, Kim, had started probate proceedings by filing the will in New York, including the filing of a document listing the value of Heath's estate to be $145,000. Larry Williams, obviously sharing at least some of the concerns raised by Heath's uncles, claimed that Heath's estate was actually worth closer to $20 million, and he called for a full disclosure of all assets. He questioned why Kim Ledger had rushed to probate court and expressed his concern that Kim should have met with his daughter's attorneys first.

Adding yet another twist to the saga, Heath's uncle, Hadyn Ledger, claimed (again publicly) that there was a "very real possibility" that Heath had another child from a relationship when he was 17 years-old.

All of this drama set the stage for a nasty family fight. But there was hope for Heath's daughter. Most states in this country offer protection for children of a parent born after a will was created under what is known as a "Pretermitted Heir" law.

However, the law often allows for only a partial inheritance in these situations. To complicate matters, Heath's will was also filed for probate in Australia, which may or may not have a similar law. Additionally, the only assets that pass pursuant to a will are those that are left in the decedent's name alone when he dies. In other words, the law may not apply at all, depending on how Heath's assets were titled (such as bank accounts, investments and life insurance).

Finally, in most states, there is no clear answer to the question of what to do with a child born before the will was created, but the father did not learn of his relationship with the child until afterwards. This may very well have been the case with Heath — if the other child was, in fact, his.

What is a pretermitted heir?

A pretermitted heir is any child or spouse who has been omitted from a will. Sometimes this omission is expressly to disinherit a potential heir, but sometimes the omission is unintentional. This could be a child that had not yet been born at the time the estate plan was written, or a spouse who married after the date of the will. Most states allow accidentally omitted children and spouses to still inherit, in some circumstances.

Luckily, it appears that the family chose not to fight over Ledger's wealth.
Kim Ledger said publicly that everything (or at least almost everything) would go to Heath's daughter Matilda.

The questions of when and how — as well as the questionable "other child" — were not answered publicly. If and when more information surfaces, we'll be sure to provide updates at TrialAndHeirs.com.

When was the last time you updated your will?

Avoid a family fight!

It seems like a basic premise which everyone would agree with, but stories like this one are all too common. Do not wait until "someday" to take care of your estate planning. Even the very young, like 28-year old Heath Ledger, need to make sure that their wishes are clearly expressed and documented. No one wants their family to face expensive, stressful, and public fights over where the money should have gone. Protect your children! Update your estate planning documents frequently, and use every legal tool at your disposal to preserve your estate for those you wish to receive it. Do not procrastinate and think that taking care of your affairs "someday" will be enough.

Chapter Five

When a loved one passes away, it usually falls to the spouse or the children to worry about the unpleasant task of administering the affairs. If you find yourself in that role, what should you do first? It's simple actually. Grieve.

Allow yourself time to value her life and recoup emotionally from the loss. You don't have to rush to an attorney. There is no need to run to court. If you lose a spouse or parent, you and the rest of the family need to come to terms with the loss as best as you can. Administering the estate can come later. A good rule of thumb, unless there are urgent matters to attend to, is two weeks, but that is just a suggestion, not a rule to live by. Keep in mind that while everyone expects some time to grieve, there are always matters to attend to — such as paying bills, collecting money, and locating assets. This can't be avoided indefinitely, no matter how hard the loss hits you.

So how long is too long? There is no exact answer. First, if you have the will but are not the person named as executor or personal representative, you must turn it over to that person, or file it with the court. Some states require this to be done within 30 days. Others have less specific laws, requiring to be done with "reasonable promptness."

If you are the person to administer the will, states vary on the length of time you have to file to open the estate. This does not mean that the estate can never be opened if you procrastinate. To the contrary, sometimes wills are probated many years after death.

However, if you do not file to open the estate promptly — in some cases, even as short as a few weeks — then creditors or others interested in the estate can force the estate to be opened. And if you are found to have waited too long, the court could determine you are not suitable to serve and appoint someone in your place to act as the executor. Generally, waiting too long will make the whole process more complicated.

When the time comes for you to proceed, what do you do?

The easiest way is to call an experienced probate attorney. An administrator's legal fees are generally paid by the estate as a whole, not the person named as executor in the will (with a few exceptions for very specific reasons). A good attorney can take care of everything for you and at no personal cost to you. If you don't want to work with an attorney and are the do-it-yourself type, then you'll need to become somewhat of an expert on probate procedures. It's not easy, but it can be done.

The not-so-basic "basics" are:

(1.) File the proper paperwork with the will or without the will if the person died intestate; (2.) Have yourself or the appropriate person appointed as executor; (3.) Serve notice on all the family members; the exact family members vary from state-to-state but at least include the spouse, children and others named in the will; (4.) Notify the known creditors; (5.) Publish a notice to unknown creditors in a local paper; (6.) Gather the assets; (7.) Pay the taxes and other debts; (8.) Address any conflicts or problems that arise; (9.) Keep the interested persons informed throughout the process; (10.) Distribute the property — which often includes selling it first and then dividing the money — and finally, (11.) Close the estate.

Sounds easy, right? Well, maybe not (unless you're a glutton for punishment). Whether you want to try it yourself will depend on how much is in the estate, whether the will is sufficiently clear, how many debts exist, whether family infighting can be expected and a number of other factors. If you want to go that route, try calling your local probate court. Each county usually has its own probate court (although some states use different names, like New York, which has Surrogate's Court). They often have brochures or guides to help walk you through the process. If not, and you still don't want to work with an attorney, there are books available to explain the process step-by-step in detail.

But no brochure or book can fully prepare you for all problems that may arise... although this book is a good start. For example, someone in the family may not like the way you handle things; such as dividing items of sentimental value. Other problems arise if someone files a legal challenge to the will. Additionally, sometimes wills or wills in conjunction with other writings are unclear or ambiguous about what was really intended.

If any of these situations arise, then it is essential to have an experienced attorney on your side. When you find yourself in a difficult situation, such as an ambiguity in the will or a family member causing trouble, remember to always err on the side of caution. It is usually safer and less expensive in the long run.

This means that when questions arise, consider bringing them to the attention of all the beneficiaries and see if they will agree, in writing, on how to resolve the problem. If that approach does not work, then formally present the problem to the probate judge assigned to the estate and seek instructions about what to do. If the judge is the one making the tough decision, then you cannot be held responsible for the decision later. The final thing to remember about serving as an estate administrator — you don't have to do it! Just because you are the one named, you can always decline if it is too difficult for you. We'll explore more of these difficulties in Chapter 21. In fact, even if you are appointed by the court to serve in that capacity, you can always change your mind and ask to be relieved of your duties.

It's not easy to be an estate administrator, especially when ambiguities and other sources of conflict arise. Don't be afraid to say "No thanks, I'll let someone else handle this one." There are many people who took on the job who certainly wish they had followed this simple advice. Sometimes estate executors are faced with very difficult situations.

the TRUE STORY
of FLO-JO

Florence Griffith Joyner was a hero of the 1988 Olympic Games. Flo-Jo, as she was affectionately called, sprinted her way to three gold medals, a world record, and the hearts of the nation. Sadly, she unexpectedly died in her sleep on September 21, 1998 at the age of 38. The cause was a severe epileptic seizure brought about from a congenital defect. It caused her to suffocate on her pillow. She left behind her husband, track star Al Joyner and her seven-year-old daughter.

Al Joyner found himself in a state of shock. He, too, had been a gold medalist in the Olympics and never imagined he would lose his wife so soon. Flo-Jo had created a will many years before, but Al Joyner did not file it with the probate court within 30 days as California law required.

Flo-Jo's side of the family grew worried. Months passed and nothing was filed. In June 1999 — almost nine months after Flo-Jo had passed — an attorney for her mother, Florence D. Griffith, filed a petition with the court. In it, Griffith asked the court to order Joyner to produce the will. Griffith was especially interested because she claimed that her daughter had promised she could reside in Flo-Jo's house for the rest of her life. Joyner had recently sued Griffith about that very issue, and had shown a copy of the will in the other legal proceeding. But he did not file the original will as he was required to do by law.

The probate judge ordered Joyner to produce the will by September 9, 1999. He was unable to do so. Instead, his lawyer filed a detailed letter Joyner had written explaining that he had been unable to locate the original will despite looking for months. He claimed it was difficult because he was consumed with caring for his daughter, opening a foundation in the name of his late wife, running a business and continuing charity work. Joyner simply could not find the will and begged the court to accept a copy instead. The judge responded by giving him another three months to continue looking.

Did Joyner ever find the will? The answer appears to be no; court records show that he never did file the will. They also reveal that he and Griffith continued to have disputes and the court ultimately appointed a neutral party to administer the estate. With all the problems it took just to get the estate started, it was no wonder that the judge removed Joyner as executor.

Eventually, the estate was resolved and the family moved on. The neutral administrator closed the estate in July 2002, almost four years after Flo-Jo passed. Who knows how much quicker and easier it would have been if Joyner had located the original will promptly?

Do your loved ones know how to find your will if you pass?

Avoid a family fight!

Al Joyner was in a difficult position that easily could have been avoided. To help your heirs avoid the same problem, make sure that at least two people you trust know where to find your original will and other estate planning documents. Leave them in a safety deposit box, fireproof safe or other secure location. You can even file your will with the local probate court for safekeeping, in many states. Some attorneys may offer to store the will for you. But, wherever you store your will, it is helpful to tell your loved ones how to reach the attorney you used so they can get in touch with him or her if tragedy strikes. The estate planning lawyer who prepared the documents can help provide copies, answer questions and maybe even represent the family in probate court if needed.

Ideas to Spark Family Discussion

The first person with whom you should have an earnest talk about your will is yourself. Do you have a will? Is it less than five years old? Has your life, since the day you signed it, been free of changes, such as a divorce, birth of a new child, or starting a business? If you answer no to any of these questions, it is time to see an attorney about preparing a will for you or at least to review the one you already have.

If you answer yes, then pull out your will and read it. Are there any confusing provisions and does your will capture all of your wishes in one place? If you feel comfortable with everything after that, make sure you store it in a safe place that your named executor and at least one other person can easily find. How can they find it? Easy — you'll tell them where to look.

Next, talk to your spouse; the same questions apply. Spouses often have wills that mirror one another, but this is not always the case. Are you recently married and feel uncomfortable bringing up this topic with your new loved one? Share some of these stories with him or her and break the ice. This topic is too important to put off for another day.

Indeed, one conversation may not be enough. Just talking about a will is not the same as creating one. If you die unexpectedly, your spouse cannot go into court and say, "Well, she told me she was going to create a will leaving everything to me." It doesn't work that way.

Next, talk to your other loved ones. Start with your parents, but don't forget about your grandparents and others you love. And simply asking, "Do you have a will?" is not enough. Tell them about Warren Burger, Heath Ledger and Sonny Bono. Make sure your parents' affairs are protected, so you don't find yourself in the same spot as the family members of these famous people, each of whom died without an adequate will.

No one who has assets and is over the age of 18 should be without a will. This is especially true for parents! They are too easy to create. Don't be afraid to talk to an attorney about one. Wills, at least for the large majority of people, are not complicated, and it is not too expensive to have done the right way. The risk of not doing so is too great.

SECTION II

If there's a will, there's a way... but there's a better way. Securing your family's future shouldn't be left to imperfection. It's far better to put your trust in trusts. Trusts help people control how, when, where and by whom their money and property should pass when they die. And here's the best part — no probate court required! But only if trusts are created and used the right way.

Chapter Six answers the basic question "WHAT IS A TRUST AND HOW DOES IT WORK?" You'll learn why they need to be crafted with care. When Ray Charles' Trust left out something important, it resulted in a family fight and unnecessary lawsuits.

In Chapter Seven you'll find out how to PUT THE FUN IN "FUNDING." Having a trust isn't enough. As Michael Jackson demonstrated, those who don't put their property into the trust during their lifetime miss out on some of the big advantages of using trusts. Even some lawyers mess up this part!

And is a trust for you? YOU MAY NEED A TRUST AND NOT EVEN KNOW IT. Chapter Eight teaches why trusts can help you whether your assets are abundant or modest. In fact, a trust very well may have saved the life of Wall Street insider and CNBC analyst Seth Tobias, whose family believes he was murdered for his money by his wife. Hopefully you'll never be in his situation, but it shows how powerful a trust can be.

Chapter Nine will help you LET YOUR CREATIVE SIDE SHOW. Trusts are not intended as "one size fits all" documents. No one's family or situation is exactly alike; neither should their trusts. But can creative trust provisions — like the "Jewish Clause" — go too far?

Finally, Chapter Ten teaches about USING TRUSTS TO AVOID CREDITORS. Sometimes you can, other times you can't. You'll learn when and why. Read the story of a CEO who dragged his family through a mountain of trouble while leveraging trusts in a dramatic chess match.

A trust is a better way to protect your legacy, your loved ones, and as The Great Stork Derby demonstrates, can help you achieve even the most unusual goals.

What exactly is a Trust?

A trust manages property on behalf of one or more individuals, whether living or deceased. It also has the power to keep family matters and finances out of probate court, and should be used in conjunction with a will to manage an estate. It is a privately managed set of instructions for assets, and although it cannot determine custody and care of minors, it can be used to apportion money and property to children and other loved ones, as well as organizations or charities.

the TRUE STORY
of THE GREAT STORK DERBY!

Trusts are an ideal way to pass along creative or detailed instructions, because they are not scrutinized by probate courts and are private. In the 1920s, a wealthy and eccentric Toronto attorney wanted just the opposite. He wanted his instructions to be very public.

Charles Vance Millar died in 1926 at the age of 73. He was never married and had no children, but he did have a large estate and a fine sense of humor. He opened his will by stating that it was "necessarily uncommon and capricious because I have no dependents or near relations." His will forewarned "what I do leave is proof of my folly in gathering and retaining more than I required in my lifetime."

Millar truly did "prove his folly." He left his valuable shares in a horse racing club to staunch opponents of gambling, just to see if their morals had a price. He bequeathed shares in a brewery to Protestant ministers and others who supported prohibition of alcohol. He gleefully willed the rights to use a vacation home in Jamaica to three attorneys who deeply disliked each other, undoubtedly to spark a fight over who got to use it and when.

But these creative clauses of craziness were just the appetizers. Canadian newspapers dubbed the main course as "The Great Stork Derby." Millar left the balance of his estate to a trust he had created, with special instructions for the trustees. They were to invest his money for nine years after his death, and on the tenth anniversary of his demise, the money and the interest it earned was to pass to "the Mother who has since my death given birth in Toronto to the greatest number of children." Millar's will and trust required that the money be divided equally if more than one mother shared the honor of most children.

But what exactly was the limit of "Toronto?" Did stillbirths count, or only live births? And what about the law that defined the word "children" in wills and trusts to exclude illegitimate children? Shouldn't those children count too? And was this whole clause even valid?

Courts wrestled with these questions for years. Distant relatives challenged this provision. Even the Province of Ontario government tried to invalidate the clause as being against the public interest. But in the end, Millar's special clause held firm. Creative and controversial as he was, Millar was allowed to leave his property as saw fit.

After years of court battles finally ended, four women claimed the grand prize. Each bore nine children through marriage during the ten years. Courts determined that other women lost because stillborn babies or children born out of wedlock did not count.

And what a grand prize it was! Because Millar had owned land in Detroit that was later chosen for the spot of the Detroit-Windsor tunnel, the cash prize was more than he could have foreseen. The winners earned $125,000 each. This was a great sum during the depression of the 1930's, when up to one in three Canadians old enough to work was unemployed. The minimum salary was only $12.50 for an entire week's worth of work. In fact, by today's standards, the prize money equals about $1.5 million each. That pays for plenty of nannies and diapers.

In addition to the obvious monetary significance to these women and their families, Millar's creative estate plan provided something else. Millions of people all across Canada followed and cheered the Great Stork Derby during a time when they desperately needed something to believe in and provide hope. Millar provided a shining example that even the most creative trusts can be valid.

How can you creatively help those you love with your estate plan?

Avoid a family fight!

Trusts solve many of the disadvantages inherent in wills, including avoiding probate court, protecting privacy, and allowing a person to leave very specific and creative directions for who should receive his or her money. While even trusts can be challenged in court, it is harder to do than for wills. Many think that if they have a will, that is all they need. As this Section discusses, for most people, a properly drafted living trust is well worth the investment.

Chapter Six

Many people hear the term "living trust" and feel overwhelmed. "I don't have an estate" they think to themselves, "Why would I need a trust? That's only for rich people." Actually, nothing could be further from the truth. The key questions to ask are: "Do I want my loved ones to be able to avoid probate court?" and "Do I want to control how my legacy is passed?"

Of course, the answers are "yes."

Let's start at the beginning. What is a trust? It is a simple concept, despite what you may have read or heard.

Have you ever hired a babysitter? When you hired one, did you open your front door and say, "I'm going to ask the third person who walks by to watch our kids when we go out tonight"? Hopefully not! You probably picked someone who you interviewed, checked a reference or two, and of course, trusted. When you were ready to go out for the evening, you left your babysitter instructions about when to put the kids to bed, how much television they could watch, and what to eat for dinner.

It's pretty basic stuff for any parent. If you can follow that, then you understand how a trust works and you probably never even realized it. In essence, a trust is nothing more than private instructions to your babysitter.

Instead of choosing someone who you trust to watch your children, you choose someone you trust to manage your assets in the event of your disability or death. You'll still need a will, or in states that allow them, a separate document setting forth your wishes to declare who should have custody of minors. Again, a trust does not address who will act as guardian to raise your children in the event you die unexpectedly. But a trust is one of the best tools for handling assets, and saying who should receive them. A trust can help with your money, home, investments and all other assets you own or acquire.

The person to trust to handle these assets when you cannot any longer (i.e., the babysitter) is called the successor "trustee." You, as the parents leaving the instructions, are the "settlors."

Settlors and Trustees

A "settlor" is the person who creates a trust. A "trustee" is the person trusted to administer the affairs of the trust, following the wishes of the settlor. One person can fill both positions; in fact, that is what most people do when they create their trusts. Once the initial settlor can no longer act as trustee (usually due to death, disability or mental incompetence), then the "successor trustee" takes over.

Instead of leaving instructions about your children's bedtime routine and meal preferences, when you create a trust, you leave detailed instructions about your assets. What property do you own? How is your money invested? Who receives the money if you pass away, and often most importantly, how do they receive it?

You determine the Who, What, Why and When. You keep complete control. Not only do you create the trust as the settlor, but you also manage all of the assets in the trust as the initial trustee. Just as important, you are the one who benefits from the trust. In other words, you are the initial beneficiary of the trust. You still control your property and money how you want.

Even if you become disabled and a new trustee fills your shoes to manage your money and pay your bills, you remain the sole beneficiary until you pass away. Once you do, the new babysitter, your successor trustee, must still follow your instructions about what to do. He or she must manage your assets for your benefit in the precise manner you wanted.

In other words, a trust created during life, when used properly, can help you both while you're alive and after you die. In fact, that is why most trusts are "living trusts."

One of the big advantages of a living trust, when used properly, is that it can avoid probate court entirely, unlike a will. In contrast, a testamentary trust does not avoid probate court and does not help during life. Because testamentary trusts aren't as useful, when we use the word "trusts" throughout this book, we mean living trusts. They are the perfect way to set forth your instructions and control your property however you want.

But be careful. Your instructions can only be followed if you accurately express them in the trust. Regardless of what you want your trust to do, a trust operates based on what it says. If your trust is incomplete, contradictory or ambiguous, your true wishes may not be fully expressed.

That's why, if you decide a trust may be for you, it is very important to work with an experienced attorney. Trusts can only help you control how your legacy is passed without the need for probate court if they are drafted and used the right way.

Trusts prepared by attorneys who aren't as experienced; or worse,

> ### Living and Testamentary Trusts
>
> *A living trust is one that is created during life and can, when used properly, help people manage their financial affairs while alive even when they are unable to do so due to advanced age, incompetence or disability. Another term for this is "inter vivos trusts," which means the same thing ("inter vivos" is Latin for "within one's life"). A testamentary trust, in contrast, is less common. It is one that is created after death, based on instructions contained within a will.*

trusts done without attorneys — usually won't help you achieve your goals. This is especially true if they leave things out, create confusion, or conflict with other documents.

the TRUE STORY
of RAY CHARLES!

No one can dispute that Ray Charles was a musical genius. In fact, Frank Sinatra dubbed him "The Genius." He produced hundreds of albums and thousands of recordings. Charles' financial legacy was valued at more than $75 million. People mourned worldwide when "The Genius" succumbed to his battle with cancer on June 10, 2004.

About eighteen months before he died, Ray Charles held a family meeting before Christmas. He invited his twelve children and their nine different mothers. He told his offspring that he knew he was dying and most of his assets were earmarked for charity. But he did not forget about them. Charles created trusts with half a million dollars for each of them, along with cash gifts of $1 million, tax free, each.

Charles also made a vague promise that they would get more "down the line." What this means has never been made clear, but Ray Charles was clear about most of his wishes. He completed extensive estate and charitable planning, complete with multiple trusts, a charitable foundation and a company called Ray Charles Enterprises. He named a long-time friend and adviser, Joe Adams, to manage it all. Adams took control of the whole ball of wax when Charles passed.

Almost four years later, several of Charles' offspring filed lawsuits against Adams.

They alleged he mismanaged Charles' legacy and his trusts, failed to disclose information, tarnished Charles' image, and even stole millions from the charitable foundation. They demanded that the Attorney General launch an investigation to protect the charities.

But perhaps most of all, the family was particularly upset with two CDs released after Charles' death which included remixed songs featuring Ray Charles paired with other singers. His children felt they had to protect their father's image which was being watered down by these CDs and other ventures.

Indeed, Ray Charles' image lay at the very heart of these disputes. The Genius's will and trusts did not address who would control the rights to his image, also known as publicity rights. For all of his extensive planning, that was one not-so-minor detail that was left out. Charles' publicity rights are important because they include the ability to market his name and likeness through t-shirts, posters, coffee mugs, sunglasses and anything else you can think of.

Ray, Jr. claimed in one of the lawsuits that his father had promised these rights to him. He even held controlling interest, at one time, in a partnership formed with his father in 1992 to sell merchandise with Charles' image. The problem was that Ray, Jr. transferred his interest in the partnership to Adams. Ray, Jr. claims that Adams refused to give him money from his father's trust which he needed to enter a drug rehab program in 2005 unless he first turned over controlling interest in the partnership.

Adams, of course, denied the claims and even filed a lawsuit of his own to keep Ray, Jr. and other family members from meddling in the matter. And perhaps Adams was right. A few months after filing the cases, the lawsuits were dismissed by the court for "lack of prosecution," in June 2008. This means that the attorney handling the cases did not do what was supposed to be done and the cases were closed.

Clearly, this wouldn't have happened accidentally. Perhaps Adams settled the claims against him with a cash payment. Perhaps he persuaded Charles' heirs that their cases had no merit. Or maybe, the lawsuits will be re-filed and the fight will continue.

Whatever the reason for the dismissal of the cases, the feud could easily have been prevented, rather simply, if Ray Charles had included clear written instructions about the rights to control his image in one of his many trusts.

Are you certain that your trust takes care of everything?

Avoid a family fight!

Trusts need to be all-inclusive to work to their fullest extent. Leaving out certain property without explanation often creates trouble. People can always argue that a valuable asset that was left out was really meant for them. If you truly want everything to pass through your trust, say so in writing. If you want something to pass another way, then mention it in the trust so there is no confusion. But make sure you are consistent. If your trust leaves a certain bank account to someone, the trust must own that account for the trust to control. If not properly included in the trust, your heirs may disagree over what you really wanted.

It is rare for a good estate planning attorney to leave something out of a trust, like what happened with Ray Charles. That's why the choice of which attorney to work with is an important one. Some people try to save a few dollars and work with the cheapest lawyer they can find. Or even worse, they prepare a trust without any attorney at all. Why is this a bad idea? Find out with this next story.

the TRUE STORY
of THE TRUST KIT NIGHTMARE!

Elizabeth was 83 years old when she first met with co-author Danielle. Elizabeth owned a condominium and several hundred thousand dollars worth of investments including stocks, bonds and insurance policies. She wanted to leave her legacy to family members including her one surviving daughter, Kathryn, and many grandchildren. But Elizabeth was worried that her daughter was not great with money and wanted to make sure her grandchildren benefitted too.

Danielle prepared a detailed trust that achieved all of Elizabeth's wishes. The trust named Kathryn's daughter, Stephanie, as the successor trustee. Danielle and Elizabeth worked together to transfer Elizabeth's bank accounts, investments and condominium into the trust.

What is a trust kit?

A "trust kit" is the grouping of pre-written forms that are created as "one size fits all." The buyer fills in a few blanks and has a trust, without meeting with an attorney. Or sometimes, a "professional" who is not an attorney does it for them. There are also many "do it yourself" kits that work the same way.

A few years later, Elizabeth accepted an invitation to attend a seminar presented by a "trust kit" company.

As you'll see, there are many drawbacks to a shortcut like using a trust kit. Elizabeth purchased the trust kit, never met with an attorney, and signed boilerplate trust documents. This new trust did not revoke or cancel the prior trust Danielle had prepared. What did this mean? Elizabeth became the proud owner of two trusts.

The new trust left all of her money, payable all at once after her death, to her daughter Kathryn. It did not leave a penny to her grandchildren. Did this represent a change of her wishes, or was Elizabeth taken in by this company without knowing what she signed? Because no attorney ever met her for the second trust, there was no one for the family to ask about what Elizabeth really intended.

Instead, after Elizabeth died, Stephanie called Andrew and Danielle's law firm. Her call was transferred to the probate litigation specialist, co-author Andrew. Andrew investigated the case and discovered what had happened with the trust kit. By the time of her death, Elizabeth had sold her condominium and most of her investments, and held all of her assets in two bank accounts, both of which were still held in the name of the first trust. The second trust held nothing.

Elizabeth had a will — also purchased through the trust kit company — which directed that any assets left in her name alone should be transferred into the second trust when she died. This, too, was unhelpful because Elizabeth died without any assets in her individual name. Instead, the entire trust kit, including the will, was nothing but a waste of Elizabeth's time and money.

Even worse, the trust kit complicated matters for the family. If the first trust had been the only one, Stephanie — as successor trustee — could have begun distributing money to the trust beneficiaries immediately. But the second trust left doubt over what Elizabeth had intended and Stephanie was forced to hold the money. The "trust kit" created enough confusion that Stephanie had to wait for the whole family to agree or obtain a court order allowing her to follow the first trust.

Eventually, the family reached a resolution, but only after many months of delay and thousands of dollars in legal fees. If Elizabeth hadn't purchased the trust kit, the family could have followed the first trust, which accurately set forth her wishes at the time.

If her wishes truly did change, she could have contacted Danielle to change her trust. Either approach would have avoided the confusion, delays and legal fees.

Do you know an experienced trust attorney, or are you planning to try a shortcut like this?

Avoid a family fight!

Don't be penny wise and dollar foolish. Many people think it will be cheaper to create a trust without paying an attorney, such as through a trust kit or a form they download from the Internet. Or they shop around for the cheapest attorneys they can find, who in turn will likely use a preprinted form.

It is far better to hire an experienced estate planning attorney instead of taking a shortcut. Everyone has individual needs, and accordingly, each trust must be designed specifically for that person.

Just like a babysitter does not treat every child exactly the same, each trustee must follow the specific instructions given for that trust. When you are the one giving the instructions, the trust must be written how you want. Read it carefully. Make sure you understand it completely. Ask questions. Verify that nothing has been left out and that your wishes are clear. Trusts that fail to properly say everything a settlor intends invite conflict down the road.

Put the "fun" in funding

Chapter Seven

Have you or your wife ever been really excited with the purchase of a new purse? Some women — and everyone knows at least one — love to buy new purses. But what good does that purse do if she never puts in her wallet, keys, makeup and other personal items? Some purses costs thousands of dollars. Why buy one if it just sits in the closet collecting dust?

This gets us to an important key to using a trust: you must transfer your assets into it. There are a few exceptions to this, addressed later, but for now remember the basic rule. A trust serves no purpose and accomplishes nothing until something — real estate, bank accounts, or other property — is placed into it. If this is never done, you can have a beautifully created, detailed set of instructions, which serves no purpose. You have an empty purse.

Let's use the example of John Smith. When John Smith hires an attorney who drafts a trust for him, John should transfer his assets into the trust. This is like moving money from one of his pant pockets conveniently labeled "John Smith" to his other pocket titled "John Smith's Trust." The money is still his, but now it is located in another one of his pant pockets. He still controls it, he still spends it how he wants, and the money is still for his benefit while he is alive.

But if John fails to transfer his money and property into the Trust pocket, then all assets that are in his name alone (the "John

Smith" pocket), must pass through probate court when John dies. Most people do not realize this. Even if John Smith has a will and a trust, his estate must still go through probate court — the very same process that he was using the trust to avoid — if the trust is not "funded." The "John Smith Trust" pocket does not work if it remains empty.

Funding

Is funding really fun? Not usually; it can be a great deal of work when someone has a lot of bank accounts, real estate and other assets. But it is important. "Funding" is the process of legally retitling and transferring assets into the name of a trust so that they are controlled by the trust's instructions.

This rule is extremely important for everyone who has a trust. Many families pay an estate planning attorney handsomely to draft a long, detailed trust. They take it home, put it away with peace of mind, not realizing that the work is not done. Once the attorney drafts the trust, the family needs to fund the trust by transferring assets into it.

Funding is not to be taken lightly, but it is not something to be afraid of either. Everyone should work with a reputable trust attorney to make sure how and when to transfer their assets into their trust. Certain assets, like IRAs, should sometimes be left outside a trust for tax reasons, and sometimes liability concerns impact when to transfer property like a home into a trust. But for the majority of bank accounts, real estate, stocks, mutual funds and insurance policies, funding is important. Often, it can be accomplished as simply as changing the title of a bank account, or by signing a deed. If you have a trust, and no one has discussed funding with you, make sure you ask a qualified attorney or financial planner experienced with funding trusts.

Sadly, you can't always count on your attorney to tell you about funding. Some attorneys purposely choose not to, to their own benefit. Why? Read on and find out.

the TRUE STORY
of A LESSON ON 'TRUST'

Many years ago, Walter and Joan, the grandparents of co-author Andrew, asked co-author Danielle to review their trusts for them. Walter was a retired pediatrician who was very sharp and quite sophisticated financially. He enjoyed investing and built an impressive portfolio. Walter and Joan spent most of their lives in Northern Indiana, before retiring to Florida, and they owned homes in both states. They worked with an estate planning attorney in Indiana whom they paid well to draft lengthy, complicated trusts, about fifty pages each.

Before Danielle even read the first word, she asked Walter and Joan if they had fully "funded" the trusts. They looked at her, confused, and asked "What on earth are you talking about?" They had not been told to transfer any of their assets into their trusts. They had expensive and well-made trust "pockets" that were empty.

When Danielle reviewed their wills, she was surprised to discover who had been named as the executor of their wills. It was their attorney — the same one who prepared their trusts. He had the hope of not only receiving payment for the trusts, but also being paid by their probate estates down the road as the executor. He never discussed funding the trusts with them.

Instead, the attorney created "pour-over wills," which are commonly done along with trusts as part of a comprehensive estate plan.

The problem is that Walter and Joan's attorney relied exclusively on the pour-over wills to accomplish funding the trusts. He never advised his clients to transfer their assets into their trusts while they were still alive.

What's a pour-over will?

Pour-over wills work by transferring all assets that remain in the name of a deceased person, through probate court, into the trust. They do this by naming the trust as the beneficiary of the will. They are a good way to fill a trust "pocket" that for one reason or another was not filled before death. But a pour-over will still needs to go through a probate court before it can "pour-over" the deceased person's assets into a trust.

If Walter and Joan had not met with Danielle, or if they were incompetent, one of the key advantages of a trust — avoiding public probate court — would have been lost.

By leaving the trust unfunded and naming himself executor of their wills, the attorney was ensuring that he'd make more money in legal fees after they died.

Luckily, both of Andrew's grandparents were clearly competent, so Danielle thwarted the attorney's nefarious plan, and worked with Walter and Joan to accomplish the funding. They transferred their home, bank accounts and other investments into the trust. Walter, now educated about using a trust, meticulously followed-up on everything to make sure that it was properly funded.

Now that many years have passed, Walter and Joan continue to enjoy good physical and mental health. They serve as their own trustees and manage their trust assets during their lifetime, and have named a family member to manage the trusts when they pass on. They preserved as much of their legacy as possible to be left to their family, who won't have to waste time or money on probate court or unnecessary attorney fees when they pass.

Are your assets funded into your trust?

Avoid a family fight!

Working with a knowledgeable attorney, fund your trusts during your lifetime. It is best to do so shortly after your trust is prepared and anytime you acquire new assets. Many probate court battles are started because assets were not transferred into the trust, but were instead left jointly with a child or in the decedent's name alone. This often leads to conflict. Once you have passed away and cannot tell people where you intended the assets to go, the family may disagree and fight over your true intent. If you place your assets into your trust when you are unquestionably still competent, your family will not need to argue about what you wanted to happen with your money and property.

the TRUE STORY
of MICHAEL JACKSON!

While there was little he could do to surprise anyone given his past eccentricities, when the King of Pop died suddenly at the age of 50 on June 25, 2009, it caught the world off guard. The circumstances surrounding Michael Jackson's death only added to the public's curiosity and intrigue. Did his doctor commit manslaughter by over medicating him? Had his advisers pushed him too hard to earn money for creditors when they knew he was too frail to survive the physical demands of a concert tour?

And, of course, everyone wanted to know what would become of his three young children whom he sheltered from the public eye while he was alive. Who would raise them? What would they inherit? Did Michael Jackson leave behind so much debt that his children would get nothing?

Before any of these questions could be answered, the probate court system first had to address who would manage his estate's financial affairs. His mother, Katherine Jackson, was first to the courthouse. She filed to open his estate on an intestate basis, reporting to the court that there was no will.

But, to her surprise, Michael Jackson did have a will. He even had a trust, the Michael Jackson Family Trust. The will named an attorney, John Branca and two others as the co-executors to manage the estate. Michael had also selected the same three to serve as co-trustees for his trust. Michael's estate plan directed that all of his assets were to pass through to this trust, through a pour-over will. Reportedly, the beneficiaries of the trust were his three children (40%), his mother Katherine (another 40%), with the rest earmarked for charity (20%).

So that ends the debate, right? He did what he was supposed to do and created a trust; what else is there?

Michael Jackson didn't do something very important: He didn't fund the trust. If he had, his affairs wouldn't have gone through the probate system at all. This mistake created a few major drawbacks for the Jackson family.

First and foremost, if he had properly funded his trust, it would have made the issue of who should administer his affairs much simpler. Once property reaches a trust, the trustee or trustees manage it outside of the public court system. But, executors of a will have to be appointed through probate court.

In this case, Michael's mother, Katherine, wasn't happy with Michael's choice of attorney, Branca, and the other non-family members. She and her attorneys initially asked the judge not to appoint them, arguing they weren't suitable to serve that important role. The judge ruled against her and appointed them as executors, but only on a temporary basis. He eventually decided Katherine could challenge them based on "undue influence" (discussed later in Chapter 15) without fear of invoking a no-contest clause (remember these from the Frank Sinatra will story?).

This leads to the second drawback. With all this uncertainty over who would administer the estate, the oversight of the probate court may last for years to come.

When Jackson's named executors came forward with the will, they filed paperwork stating his estate had assets worth approximately $500 million. But that's simply an initial estimate. With all of his existing music royalty rights and future business endeavors capitalizing on his music, name and image, that total will surely climb significantly as time passes. Think of it this way, Michael's name and image could be licensed to makers of anything from gloves to movies, and royalties for this "usage" would make additional revenue for the Jackson Estate. But someone has to decide which deals to accept and which to reject. That's the job of the executors.

Opportunities came fast and furious. Right off the bat, the executors negotiated with Sony to sell his concert tour rehearsal video for a reported $50 million. Katherine Jackson wanted a say in these negotiations, too. The judge ruled she could challenge decisions like the Sony deal.

In fact, anytime the heirs didn't agree with the co-executors' choices, they simply had to appear before the probate judge and complain. In addition to the increased legal fees and time spent in court, this gave the media and the public more opportunities to watch everything that happened. For example, the executors had to obtain approval from the judge for an allowance for Katherine and Michael's children, so the press was treated to knowing how much they needed to live on (a whopping $86,000 per month, not counting housing expenses, if you're curious) and details like Katherine's $1,000 monthly bill for "grooming."

With a properly-funded trust, this very public probate court oversight would not have been needed. The same people would have made these same decisions, but they would have done so as "trustees" and therefore a judge's approval would not have been required. It would have been much harder for Katherine Jackson or anyone else to challenge those decisions.

So instead of saving legal fees and keeping his financial affairs private, Michael Jackson did just the opposite. He subjected his children, mother, and executors to repeated court hearings.

Although critical mistakes were made, it is difficult to fault Michael for this, because he may have been depending on the advice of his counsel.

The Michael Jackson case is a story that is sure to take many turns. You can sign up at TrialAndHeirs.com for the latest developments.

Have you made sure that your affairs will remain private and out of court after you pass on?

Avoid a family fight!

It's very important to select a trustee who you trust to manage your affairs responsibly and fairly for all beneficiaries. Because trusts are managed outside of court supervision, unlike estates, the trustees have a great deal of freedom and control. Without an existing court process to oversee them, there is a greater chance for abuse. So choose wisely... select a trustee that you trust.

And be wary of the choices Michael Jackson made. Except for those who have an unusually trusting relationship with their estate planning attorney, it is usually not advisable to choose your attorney to also serve as your trustee. In Jackson's case Branca was the attorney who prepared his will and trust — and now serves as a trustee over the trust. Some would say it is ethically blurry for attorneys to suggest to clients that they name them as executor or trustee.

Why? Doing so may result in financial gain for the attorney, especially if the family has to take extra trips to probate court that could have been avoided. Branca is well respected in entertainment circles, so it would be a big surprise if he intended this result. But if your attorney suggests that they serve as your executor or trustee, think twice before proceeding with them.

So did Branca advise Michael to fund his trust and Michael ignored his instructions? Or did Branca conveniently "forget" to tell him about the funding requirement so he could receive more money in legal fees, just like the lawyer in the story about Andrew's grandparents? Is it possible that Katherine's allegation of undue influence was based on similar speculation? Again, it would be a surprise in Hollywood if that was the situation with Branca.

You may need a trust and not even know it

Chapter Eight

Now you know what a trust is, how it works, and the importance of funding it. But the big question remains: Is a trust right for you? Is it worth your time — and more importantly — is it worth spending your money to meet with an attorney to prepare a trust?

Many people, including many with substantial assets, mistakenly think it's not worth their time or money. In fact, most people spend more time and money planning a vacation each year than they do preparing an estate plan. But don't fall into this way of thinking, a vacation is short-lived, but matters of your estate will affect your loved ones for the rest of their lives and beyond.

For many, creating a trust is essential. Trusts are a great way to minimize estate taxes. Did you think that you may not need to worry about estate taxes because they only apply to very large estates? If so, you may be surprised one day.

Think of it this way: Estate taxes are the government's way of earning income at the expense of wealthier citizens and their families. If you pass away and you own enough assets and money to reach the dollar level set for the year you die, then your estate will have to pay estate taxes to the government. The price tag: about 50 percent of every dollar you have that is over the level. That's right, a big chunk of your hard-earned money could go to the government by the "death tax" as some call it. And the dollar figure set for this changes, sometimes on a yearly basis.

These inheritance taxes are a concern for many more people than you may realize. Life insurance counts towards this limit, as does the equity in your house and the value of all other assets you own when you pass. So many of us have assets that are worth more at the time of our death than during our lifetime. With the uncertain political climate in this country, you never know when the laws may change and suddenly you may have enough assets to require an estate tax to be paid when you die. Anyone with sufficient assets that estate taxes might apply someday should create a trust with the help of an experienced estate planning attorney to minimize these taxes. For these people, trusts are essential.

Trusts are also crucial for certain parents. Do you, or anyone you know, have a child with special needs? Does that child receive governmental assistance such as Medicaid or supplemental security income benefits?

Parents of these children must have a properly drafted trust... but one different than most trusts. These parents need a special needs trust.

Special needs trusts are important because governmental benefits are limited — if someone has assets of a certain level, they lose their benefits. This level is quite low; generally, it is only $2,000. A special needs trust prepared by an experienced attorney offers the perfect solution. But a big word of caution. Not all estate planning lawyers are experienced in creating special

Special Needs Trust

A "special needs trust" is a very important type of trust that is used by people who want to leave money or property to someone, often a child, who receives certain governmental benefits (such as Medicaid or SSI) because of a medical condition or disability. Many parents of these special children are afraid to leave them anything for fear of losing these benefits. But a special needs trust (when done correctly) will allow them to keep their benefits and still receive an inheritance.

Section II | Chapter Eight

needs trusts. A simple misstep in creating the document can cause a child to lose all benefits. It is more important for these parents — more so than anyone else — to work with an attorney experienced in special needs trusts. The cost of not doing so can be truly devastating if any mistakes are made.

What about everyone else? What if you don't have a special needs child and aren't concerned with estate taxes in the future. Do you still need a trust? Is it worth the expense?

For most people, the answer is still yes, but it depends on your goals. Do you want your family to avoid the expense and aggravation of probate court? Do you want to keep your affairs private after you pass away? Are you worried that your family may fight over your assets when you are gone? Do you have special concerns over leaving money to someone that may not be mature enough to handle it? Do you have a loved one with drug or alcohol issues?

If you answer "yes" to any of these questions, even if you do not have a large financial net worth, you should meet with a qualified estate planning attorney and discuss whether a trust is right for you. A well drafted trust can satisfy all of these concerns and more.

But do you really need an attorney to avoid probate court? Can you get by without paying a lawyer? Some people think so. They think that they can take a shortcut.

For example, they may add a child's name to the deed of their house to avoid probate court. At first blush, this might sound clever. If you pass away and your daughter's name is on the title to your house with you, then that house might not have to pass through probate court.

Unfortunately, this approach leads to a long list of potential problems that are discussed in Chapter Sixteen. Do you want your child's creditors to try to take your savings? Do you want to lose control of your property? Do you want your family to fight over whether your daughter — whose name is on the deed — gets to keep the house or share it with your other children? If you answer "Heck No!" to any of these questions, you probably should not place a family member's name on your assets to avoid probate court. At the very least, you should read Section IV carefully.

Nothing works as well as a trust to accomplish all of your objectives without the myriad of potential problems that a shortcut creates. For everyone from the very wealthy to those who are only moderately comfortable, there are too many hidden dangers and costs down the road. A good trust can avoid them, and offer many more advantages.

the TRUE STORY
of THE WEALTHY HEDGE FUND MANAGER WHO DROWNED!

Seth Tobias seemingly had it all — a beautiful wife, an estate valued between $25 million to $45 million, his own quarter-billion-dollar Wall Street hedge fund company, and regular appearances on CNBC as a financial expert. He enjoyed fame, fortune and respect; yet he drowned in the pool of his $5 million home in West Palm Beach, Florida on September 4, 2007. He was only 44 years old. The circumstances surrounding his death were strange, to say the least. His wife of 2½ years, Phyllis, called a friend after seeing him floating in the pool. She reportedly then waited 30 minutes to call 911. By the time the police arrived, Seth had been dead for so long that his body was already stiff with rigor mortis.

The toxicology report on his body showed cocaine and sleeping pills. Seth had been Phyllis' fourth husband... she was his first wife. Because of the death, she became very wealthy. But, despite all his financial expertise and stock-market savvy, Seth never did the basic estate planning that most wealthy people do. He never created a trust. Instead, he only had an old will, leaving his money to his brothers, friends and charitable causes. Seth never updated the will after he married Phyllis. Luckily for Phyllis, this meant she took the entire estate.

Under Florida's law, a spouse who is not mentioned in a will shares in the estate. This falls under the "pretermitted heir" law discussed in Chapter Four, where a spouse or child is left out of a will. In other words, the law assumes that a husband would have left his money to his wife, and the court will, in essence, rewrite the will if it fails to leave something to the spouse, unless it specifically disinherits her. In cases like this one, when the husband has no children, the wife gets it all.

Seth's brothers were bothered by the manner in which he died. They seized upon allegations by an Internet psychic who gave advice to Phyllis on a daily basis. This man screamed publicly that Phyllis had confessed to him that she laced Seth's pasta that night with cocaine and sleeping pills... and then encouraged him to enter the pool so she could kill him. The publicity-seeking psychic even claimed that Phyllis lured Seth into the pool with a promise that she would watch him have sex with a male stripper named Tiger. (Yes, ugly rumors and innuendos like this do get brought up in court fights... all the more reason to keep things private!)

The police doubted the psychic's story, especially given his past as a criminal con man. And we thought Internet psychics were a trusted source of information!

Of course, this psychic did have some evidence to corroborate his story, including the toxicology report, the manner in which Phyllis waited to call the police on the night Seth died, and the fact that Seth and Phyllis fought often — physically and verbally.

Slayer Statute

Most states have laws called "slayer statutes" that are written to prevent people from murdering someone in order to receive an inheritance. Whenever someone is killed, if the killer did so unlawfully (in other words, self defense, and accidents usually don't count), then that killer forfeits his or her inheritance.

In fact, Seth had even filed for divorce once and threatened to do so again, many times. Plus, Phyllis's phone records showed she spoke to this psychic very often, paying him thousands each month for his advice.

So Seth's family sued Phyllis. Florida, like most other states, has a law called the Slayer Statute which does not allow a person who intentionally kills someone to inherit from the estate.

Seth's family used this law to try to keep Phyllis from receiving any of Seth's money or property. If they convinced the jury that she killed Seth, his family would win, even though Phyllis was never charged criminally. Just like with the O.J. Simpson case, a civil or probate court can determine someone unlawfully killed another even without a criminal conviction.

In June 2008, the two sides settled on the eve of trial. Phyllis kept most of the estate, but Seth's family and other beneficiaries of the will received several million dollars, Seth's New Jersey condominium and his hedge fund business on Wall Street. Phyllis kept the Florida properties and many millions more. Despite the resolution, the family refused to retract their allegations of murder against Phyllis.

Only Phyllis knows for certain if these allegations are true. *Do you wonder how a trust could have impacted this case?*

Avoid a family fight!

Seth made a mistake that most people would not suspect of a financially savvy investment guru... he never created a trust. Florida's pretermitted spouse law that allowed Phyllis to take his estate, despite not being mentioned in his will, does not apply to living trusts. If Seth had created and funded a living trust, even if it predated the marriage and failed to mention his wife, everything in the trust would have passed to the beneficiaries Seth named. Yes, Phyllis would have been left out altogether.

If you believe that Phyllis really did kill him, think about this — if Seth had a properly-funded trust, then she would not have financial motive to murder him. In other words, a good trust could have saved his life!

Even if you don't think there was foul play involved, the fact remains that no one with even a fraction of Seth's wealth and financial expertise should be without a trust. He, not the law of the state where he lived, should have been able to direct where his money went. He could have passed his property on to Phyllis, his brothers and anyone else he wanted with a trust.

the TRUE STORY
of THE DISINHERITED CHILD!

You definitely do not need to be a millionaire like Seth Tobias to benefit from a trust.

Several years ago, Danielle met with a new client, Rebecca, who had a modest estate consisting of some money market accounts and a condominium. In total, her assets scarcely totaled over $150,000.

Rebecca was 78 years old and divorced. She had two children: a daughter that she was very close to and a son that she had not spoken to in years.

Rebecca's primary concern was making things as easy as possible on her daughter upon her passing. This was especially important because she did not want her son to receive a cent. Her daughter had been there for her, regularly helped her out, and they enjoyed a strong bond.

The problem was that if Rebecca only had a will, then her daughter would have to file it with the probate court upon her death. Even though her son would be disinherited, he would still receive a letter informing him when the estate was opened, as well as a copy of the will.

This would open the door for a will contest, and Rebecca was very worried that is exactly what her son would do. But Danielle solved this problem with a trust.

By preparing a living trust, Danielle helped Rebecca achieve her goals. Her daughter would be the only beneficiary, and even as trustee, she would have no obligation to provide anything to her brother — not even a copy of the trust — because he was not a beneficiary.

Rebecca did not have to worry about her daughter going to probate court when she died and inviting trouble from her son.

Have you done everything you can to help prevent a family fight over your assets when you're gone?

Avoid a family fight!

Because a son or daughter who is not a trust beneficiary has no right to receive a copy of the trust, that person has a much more difficult time contesting the document. Why? The trust can be administered and the person who was cut out will not even know what happened. This does not work with wills, which by law must be provided to all children, even if not included. Those who use a trust, like Rebecca, will have peace of mind knowing that their intended beneficiaries will receive the estate after death and most likely avoid a court fight.

Let your creative side show

Chapter Nine

Turn your thoughts back, once again, to the last time you remember hiring a babysitter. But think of the time when you hired a new one who did not already know your children well. When that happened, did you let someone else give you a couple choices of what instructions to leave? Did you check a few boxes and leave it at that? Bedtime is at eight. Dinner at seven. Bath or no bath. Television limited to sixty minutes or no television at all. That may cover the basics, but not everything for your unique child.

What did you tell the babysitter if one of your children had a food allergy or was often sick? What if a child was not allowed to watch a certain scary movie on television that night? What if one child wanted pepperoni pizza, the next child wanted cheese only, and the third child wanted a peanut butter and jelly sandwich with the crusts cut off after the bread was toasted and shaped into triangles, along-side her Elmo bowl filled to the rim with the curly pretzels, but not the straight ones?

If that happened, you told the babysitter exactly what you wanted done, how it should be done, and when. You gave explicit instructions. If needed, you were creative. You were detailed. You made sure she knew exactly what your wishes were.

A good trust can work exactly the same way. The benefits of a trust far exceed avoiding probate court and reducing family conflict. The trust can reach as far as your imagination allows.

What if your children have vices that you don't like? You certainly would not want your legacy to be thrown away through gambling, drinking or drug use. A trust can limit distributions to beneficiaries who are sober, and can even require drug screenings to prove it.

Is it possible that you may want to include someone who is not good with money? You can tailor a trust to distribute money to him or her over time, and only if certain conditions are met. You can even take the discretion away completely and leave the money in the hands of a separate trustee who directly pays appropriate expenses of your beneficiary. If your son who likes to throw money away presents a valid bill, or asks for money to buy a respectable house, then your trustee can pay it, but only if you gave the trustee discretion or authority to do so.

What if there is a second marriage? How do you maintain the lifestyle of the new spouse but preserve a legacy to leave to the children of the first marriage? You guessed it... a trust. Often, the trust will allow the spouse to use the income from the assets during his or her life, and the children receive the remaining assets when the spouse passes away. But each family and each situation is different, and so is each trust.

You can decide that your children have enough money, and instead create a trust that benefits your grandchildren, but only if they finish college first. You can leave money to charities, political causes, friends, distant relatives, and anyone else you wish — and tie whatever strings you want to the money. If you are worried about your son getting divorced, you can leave money in the hands of a trustee and not give direct access to your son.

A good trust can accomplish all of these things. As long as the trust settlor is competent, and accurately expresses his or her wishes in the trust, anything that is not illegal is possible. Well... almost anything. There are exceptions, in some states.

the TRUE STORY
of THE JEWISH CLAUSE

Max Feinberg was raised in an Orthodox Jewish family during the 1910's and 20's. When he attended dental school as one of only a few Jewish students, he endured anti-Semitic slurs. He persevered during the Great Depression — working seven days a week — and built a successful dental practice. Because of his hard work, Feinberg enjoyed financial success and built an estate worth millions. Throughout it all, he took his Jewish faith and legacy very seriously.

When Feinberg created his estate plan with the help of a Chicago attorney, he included a very unusual provision in his trust. It said that any grandchild or great-grandchild of his would lose all inheritance rights if the person married outside the Jewish faith. Well, he was a little flexible... it went on to say that they could retain their inheritance rights if their spouse converted to Judaism before their 1st anniversary.

It came to be known as the "Jewish Clause." It meant that his five grandchildren would lose $250,000 (the amount he left to each of them) if they married the "wrong" person.

His grandchildren had different perspectives about the clause. All were highly educated (Feinberg's trust also paid for their college educations), and one who married outside the Jewish faith was a financially successful doctor. He wasn't deterred in marrying the woman he loved even though it cost him one-quarter of a million dollars.

Another grandchild had a different view. Michele Trull also married a non-Jewish person. But she didn't accept the disinheritance. Instead, she sued her father and others in charge of Feinberg's estate and trust, and asked the court to disregard the Jewish Clause because she felt it violated public policy in the state of Illinois.

The trial judge agreed with Trull. He ruled that Trull's inheritance couldn't be lost simply because she married a non-Jewish husband. Trull's father and others appealed the decision to the Illinois Court of Appeals.

The three appellate judges who ruled on the case had differing views. One felt it was a simple matter — prior case law held that any will or trust clause that interfered with someone's right to marry whomever they wanted was invalid. A second agreed with that ruling, but wrote a separate legal opinion discussing how he feared that if the clause were upheld, it would encourage "the worst bigotry imaginable." While Feinberg may have had noble intent, what would happen when someone wanted to prevent marrying someone Jewish, or for that matter, any sanction against marriage outside of a common faith, race or ethnicity?

The final judge wrote that the case should be decided differently. He respected Feinberg's desire to preserve a 4,000 year old heritage, which many feel needs protecting in light of the strong antisemitism and bigotry that occurred throughout the world during Feinberg's life. He also felt that while the clause may be prejudicial, it was Feinberg's money, and he had the right to be prejudicial if he wanted to when deciding how to give it away.

But that wasn't the end of the Jewish Clause or the family fight. The case was appealed again to the highest court in the state (the Illinois Supreme Court). All seven justices (which is what judges who sit on a supreme court are called) ruled the same way. They reviewed the case and disagreed with the two lead judges from the Court of Appeals. In other words, they upheld the principles of the Jewish Clause. They believed that Feinberg and his wife (who followed her husband's wishes in the trust after he died even though she could have chosen not to) had the right to leave their money "as they saw fit and to favor those grandchildren of whose life choices they approved" under the circumstances of that case.

Like many decisions from state supreme courts, this one was a great deal more complex than we can get into here (without boring you to tears). In the end, however, the Feinbergs got their way.

Whether you believe Max Feinberg went too far or not, you do have to give him credit for one thing. He certainly was creative with his trust.

How creative do you want to be with your estate planning wishes, to reflect your unique values, beliefs and concerns?

Avoid a family fight!

When your attorney prepares a trust with an unusual feature, it helps to include an explanation directly in the trust. People affected by a clause that may not seem rational to them will be much more accepting if they understand why. Doing so will also help to dissuade a legal challenge in court. A legitimate reason included in the trust explaining that unconventional provision helps show that the settlor was in his right mind and fully understood what he did. When something that appears strange is included without an explanation, it may appear that the settlor did not have all of his faculties. In reality, the person may simply have been crazy like a fox. If Feinberg had left more details about why he felt so strongly about protecting his Jewish heritage, perhaps the many judges reading it would have an easier time upholding it. Some have questioned why he only limited his grandchildren from marrying outside his faith, and not his children. Others said if he really wanted to protect his faith, why not preclude his heirs from converting to a different religion? While the Jewish Clause won out in the end, perhaps the fight could have been avoided if it was written differently.

the TRUE STORY
of THE HARD WORKING PLUMBER!

Trusts can be creative without being as controversial as Feinberg's trust. Many years ago, George came to Andrew and Danielle's law firm for estate planning and met with their partner Don. George was 82 and was proud of his legacy. He worked hard, starting with nothing, and built a successful plumbing company from the ground up. Every day of his life, until he retired, he devoted himself to his business with long hours and extreme pride. He was rewarded with financial security for his entire family.

When it was time to decide how to pass on the fruits of his labor, he realized his children did not need the money. Due to his years of hard work, all of his children enjoyed fine educations and were successful. Instead, he wanted to help his grandchildren.

But George was very worried; he didn't want them to inherit the money and grow lazy. So it was recommended that he consider a trust with a special provision that George liked very much.

Each of his grandchildren would have to present their tax returns to the trustee in April of every year. Every dollar that they earned was matched by the trust. The trust included exceptions for good reasons, like military service or stay-at-home moms. But for most of the grandchildren, the incentive to work hard like their Grandfather George was provided.

George could pass along his proud legacy to his family and rest easy in his golden years knowing that his grandchildren would benefit from the money instead of growing complacent. George's creativity allowed him to achieve his important wish and still leave his money to his grandchildren.

Do you have children or others you want to leave money to that may not be ready to handle it?

Avoid a family fight!

Don't think that you have to leave your money to your heirs all at once... payable immediately on death. It's your money; give it to them as you see fit. You can use your money to encourage your loved ones to get an education, buy a home or change their lives.

Not everyone needs this type of encouragement, but take the time to think it through. People who receive money they are not ready for often find themselves in trouble. Your family may thank you even more in the long run if you protect those who need it from themselves.

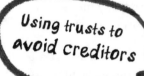
Using trusts to avoid creditors

Chapter Ten

Have you ever lost sleep at night because debt collectors hounded your son or daughter? Or instead did you lie awake because you had too much debt of your own? Ever wondered if a trust can help?

Sometimes, it can. But anyone who hopes to use a trust as a shield against creditors needs to understand exactly what it can and cannot do. There are times when trusts can be used to avoid creditors, but only sometimes.

Creditors, divorce, and poor spending habits can cause concern that heirs may not receive money intended for them. When trust settlors want to leave money to someone but have these concerns, a trust can help. Distribution provisions may be set up to pay out the money over time, when certain conditions are met, or only as needed for specific reasons (education, buying a new home, etc.). But this will only help protect your assets in a trust from passing into the hands of your beneficiaries' creditors, if your trust contains a "spendthrift" clause.

A spendthrift clause only works if the trust is properly written and if the money is not left for the beneficiary

Spendthrift clause

A "spendthrift clause" is special language contained in a trust that states that the money and other property held in a trust is to be held for the benefit of the beneficiaries and not their creditors. If worded properly, at least in most states, this clause will protect the beneficiaries so their creditors do not receive the money before they do.

in a "lump sum;" in other words, all at once. Creditors cannot reach any money remaining in the trust. It saves the beneficiaries from themselves.

But a trust is not a tool to hide from creditors or avoid paying legitimate debts. Once distributions are made, and the money leaves the trust, it is no longer protected and is subject to the debt of the beneficiary who receives the money.

But what about your own debts? Can you avoid those with a trust? Many people try. They create a trust and put all their assets into it. "It's not my money," they argue, "it belongs to the trust." This approach doesn't usually work.

Revocable vs. Irrevocable trusts

Most trusts are "revocable," meaning the settlor can change or cancel it, while he or she is alive and competent. An "irrevocable" trust, on the other hand, is one that cannot be changed or canceled even by the person who created it. That's why they are rarely used, except in specific circumstances where they are required (such as for certain tax reasons).

There are limited times when it may help, at least in some states. Usually, this requires the trust to be "irrevocable."

While making a trust irrevocable can sometimes help with creditors, that fact alone is not enough. In addition, the trustee must be someone other than the settlor, along with certain other conditions. But even then, if the purpose is to hide debt or avoid creditors, or if using the trust leaves a person with more debt than assets, then courts can and do ignore the trust and allow the creditors to be paid. Often in these cases, the trust does nothing more than increase legal fees.

No one should ever try to use a trust to protect against liability or creditors without first consulting with a knowledgeable attorney. And even then, proceed with caution.

the TRUE STORY
of THE CEO WHO PLAYED CHESS
WITH TRUSTS!

In 1979, Stephen C. Hilbert founded Conseco, an insurance and financial services giant. The company grew into a Fortune 500 company, with billions in yearly revenues. Through the 1990s, Hilbert enjoyed a lavish lifestyle from his Conseco earnings. As the CEO, he lived in a $25 million estate named "Le Chateau Renaissance." He owned an 18,500 square-foot ocean-front home in the Caribbean, along with racehorses in Kentucky, valuable artwork and Ferraris. He earned $119 million in 1997 alone.

Hilbert married his sixth wife, an exotic dancer named Tomisue who was 25 years his junior. In fact, he named his first racehorse "Tomisue's Delight." But Hilbert sought even more. He borrowed $175 million from Conseco, mostly to purchase more stock in the company. But suddenly, the market turned.

Due to some decisions that Hilbert made, Conseco began to suffer in dramatic fashion. The value of Conseco's stock crashed from $58 a share down to a mere nickel. Conseco eventually had to file for bankruptcy. The company's debt far exceeded its assets.

In 2000, Conseco forced Hilbert to accept a buy-out; the company he built into a multi-billion dollar entity kicked him out the door. Even worse, the stock he purchased was almost worthless, yet Hilbert still owed Conseco $200 million in unpaid loans.

Shortly thereafter, Hilbert began transferring almost all of his assets into trusts in the name of Tomisue, which were for the benefit of Tomisue, as well as Hilbert's children. He worked with highly paid attorneys to try to protect his assets from Conseco. There was too much money to hide under the mattress.

When these trusts were discovered, Conseco did not hesitate. It filed a lawsuit against Hilbert, Tomisue, and even Hilbert's two minor children, seeking to set aside the transfers to the trusts and to collect on the unpaid loans. Conseco's lawyers contended the trusts were a sham.

Hilbert fought back, arguing in court that the trusts and the asset transfers were legitimate. He wasn't trying to hide assets, he claimed, he merely wanted his ex-stripper wife to use the trusts for valid reasons. For example, he argued that she was an astute businesswoman who needed financing to sell purses and other women's clothing and accessories. (Anyone buy that excuse?) Hilbert complained to the press that the company was merely out to destroy his reputation and attack his young children.

In the end, Hilbert and Conseco settled. In December 2006, the lawsuit was fully and finally resolved. The settlement terms have never been made fully public, but Conseco immediately received the $25 million estate home, and sold Stephen and Tomisue Hilbert's furniture, artwork and antiques for more than $10 million, through Sotheby's auction house.

Did the trusts allow Hilbert and his family to save some of his fortune, once estimated to be more than $400 million? We do not know for sure. We do know that he lost most of his assets and spent countless dollars on legal fees — likely reaching into the millions. He paid attorney after attorney, desperately fighting to uphold the trusts that he had once hoped would save him from the company he built. The trusts he hid behind did not save his house, furniture or his lifestyle. They certainly did not spare him the humiliation and embarrassment of a vicious and well-publicized court battle into which even his young children were dragged.

Are you using your trust for the right reasons?

Avoid a family fight!

Trusts can be used to make sure that your inheritance is left for your beneficiaries and not their creditors, when used correctly. However, some people think they can escape from their own debts by hiding their assets in trusts. This strategy usually does not work. A trust can often be part of a valid plan to reduce liability, but no one should have the false sense of security that putting their money into a trust means that they will not have to pay debts they owe. That's not what trusts are for.

Ideas to Spark Family Discussion

Trusts are the backbone of any estate plan for people with significant assets or valid concerns about probate court, family conflict, children who need extra help, or many other reasons. The first step is to ask your aging parents or other family members: Do you have a trust?

If not, you now can explain in simple terms what a trust is, how it works, and why they would benefit by having one. You can tell your family that a will is usually not enough, and simply adding names to the deed or bank accounts will likely cause more trouble than it is worth. Your parents owe it to their family and their legacy to make sure their wishes are preserved and honored the right way.

If your parents do have a trust: Have they updated it recently? Did a respected attorney prepare it or was it created through a trust kit? Have they put the original in a safe deposit box, or somewhere else safe so their children can locate it after they're gone? A trust that no one can find does not do much good.

Ask your family members if they will share with you the name of the attorney who prepared it in case you have questions in the future. That way, if you cannot find a copy of the trust after they pass, you can contact the attorney who prepared it and obtain the trust. You can also do some research about the attorney and make sure that he or she is reputable.

In most situations, you shouldn't ask how or to whom your parents choose to leave their money. This may cause them to say: "That's none of your business!" Let them decide what instructions to leave and how to pass on their legacy. But it is important that they have done it, and done it properly.

If your loved ones are receptive to help and have not recently seen a good attorney, you can offer to help them find one. But let them talk to the attorney alone. The attorney will help your parents; let them be free to make their own decisions. Your very presence in the room with the attorney may appear to outsiders to be an attempt at influence. If you introduce them to an experienced and reputable attorney, you have done your job.

It is often not easy to raise these issues with your parents or other family members. Many are private and insistent upon keeping control — to the point that they refuse to discuss their plans with their children. Tell them that you only want them to make sure their wishes are preserved and followed, and it is completely up to them what their wishes are. If your parents still are not open to a dialogue, lend them this book, and let them see for themselves the importance of creating a trust with the help of a good estate planning attorney.

SECTION III

PEOPLE ARE CRAZY, RELATIVELY SPEAKING

A different twist on the "where there's a will, there's a way" saying is one favored by many estate planning and probate attorneys...

"Where there's a will, there's a relative."

Money can bring out the worst in people. It is especially true for people who are counting on someone to die so they can get their hands on an inheritance. Sometimes, people see an opportunity in an elderly family member. Other times, it is a caregiver or unscrupulous member of the opposite sex. Regardless of the reasons why, when a person is dismayed by an estate plan, what is there to do about it?

The first thing is to ask yourself is, "IS IT WORTH THE FIGHT?" As you'll learn from Chapter Eleven, a will or trust contest is never easy. But it can certainly be worth it. Take the case of Asia's richest woman. Did she really intend to leave all of her billions to her former feng shui master?

But, of course, the choice to enter a will contest depends on what legal rights you have. A good probate lawyer will tell you that the first question of whether a will or trust is valid is based on the "formalities." It's more than just DOTTING THE 'I'S AND CROSSING THE 'T'S. Chapter Twelve will teach you what lawyers look for, using a classic example of a husband and wife who accidentally signed each other's wills instead of their own.

And that's just the start. The most common question in these legal disputes arises when it seems MOM WASN'T IN HER RIGHT MIND. Chapter Thirteen discusses how the law views the question of whether the person who signed the will or trust was mentally capable of understanding what he or she signed. The war over the Johnson & Johnson family fortune addressed this very question, after a will left it all to a maid-turned-wife. And this concept also led to one of the more intriguing criminal trials New York has ever seen, in the Brooke Astor case.

HOW DOES THIS WORK IN THE REAL WORLD? Chapter Fourteen will help. The legal test for mental competency is one thing. The practicalities of winning a case turn on the evidence. So how do you know if there is enough evidence? Consider the quirky wishes of Leona Helmsley, which were challenged by her grandchildren because of Helmsley's unusual love of dogs.

But, the competency question doesn't end the intrigue. Sometimes even a competent person is tricked or badgered into signing a will or trust that he or she wouldn't have otherwise signed. This is another reason to sue, explored in Chapter Fifteen: UNDUE INFLUENCE — ABUSING THE TRUST. And you won't believe what a nurse in Michigan did to convince her boyfriend to leave her everything.

In fact, that case was almost as heated as the fights surrounding the James Brown Estate.

the TRUE STORY
of JAMES BROWN!

The Godfather of Soul died during the early morning hours of Christmas Day, 2006. The fireworks surrounding his estate began to erupt quickly. Brown left behind at least four women he was married to at different times, along with six children through marriage and three other children who may or may not have been fathered by Brown. Yes, he was a busy man!

Brown had made plans for his children — well, most of them at least. In 2000, he created a will covering his personal property. He then used a different estate planning attorney to create an irrevocable living trust to pass his musical legacy, image rights, businesses and his South Carolina Island estate to charity to benefit underprivileged students. His total estate was valued at around $80 million, but with substantial debt. Of course, the value would grow significantly with proper management of his image and song rights.

Some of his children were not happy with so much of his property passing to charity. Others wanted to honor his wishes. Some challenged the trustee and estate administrators for improper management. They even fought over where and how to bury his body (it was temporarily buried at the home of one of his daughters). Enough to keep those probate lawyers busy? Wait, there's more.

Brown's last wife was named Tomi Rae Hynie, and she married him five years before he died. The problem was that Hynie was still technically married to a

Pakistani man whom she claimed wed her only to earn a Green Card. That marriage was eventually annulled after her marriage to Brown. Brown reportedly was very unhappy when he learned about it, and announced in August 2003 that he and Hynie were separating.

So it seemed Brown did not want to leave anything to Hynie. She was not mentioned in the will or trust. Neither was her son, James Brown II. But the will and trust were created before he married Hynie and before James II was born. In South Carolina, like most states, when a spouse or child come along after a will or trust is created, the family members get a share in the estate and trust, unless the estate planning document(s) expressly disinherited them. Again, that "pretermitted heir" statute rears its head. So of course, this gave Hynie and James II good grounds to add yet another lawsuit to the James Brown Estate Battle.

But two big questions remained. Could Hynie qualify for this legal right when the marriage may not have been valid? And the second question, apparently first raised by Brown himself before he died, was James II really his son?

Brown's estate administrators apparently felt the marriage and son were not legitimate. When they filed documents to probate Brown's will, they omitted any reference to a wife, marriage, or son named James Brown II. In fact, Hynie alleged they locked her out of the "marital home" depriving her and her son of their belongings. Yet another reason to sue!

With all these claims, lawsuits, allegations and innuendos, the attorneys worked out a comprehensive settlement. The feuding family members agreed that 50 percent of Brown's property and rights would go to charity as he wanted, 25 percent to Hynie (with an acknowledgment that she was a lawful widow), and the final quarter passing to Brown's adult children. The settlement also recognized James II as a legitimate child and heir.

The judge, after months of deliberation and questioning the fairness of the settlement, approved it and allowed the compromise to stand. He also ruled that the family had to create a museum or memorial to properly lay Brown's body to rest.

Yet, despite this global resolution, the fighting still continued. Former Brown trustees asked the judge to reconsider the ruling and deny the settlement. Additionally, a few claims previously dismissed, including lawsuits by a former administrator and a disgruntled employee, are still in dispute and will bounce around the court of appeals for years to come.

Be sure to check TrialAndHeirs.com periodically for any new developments to emerge in this story.

Have you considered the difficult family dynamics between step-parents and step-children that can impact your estate after you've passed?

Avoid a family fight!

Second marriages (and third, and fourth marriages) are often magnets for trouble when it comes to legal fighting over wills, trusts and estates. That's why, in those cases, it is extra important for both spouses to be careful and thorough with their estate planning. When the wills and trusts are outdated, or non-existent, there is almost always an invitation to fight. Spous-es and children of prior marriages often do not get along but hold their emotions in check out of love and respect for the parent/spouse. Once that person dies, the emotions can easily boil over, increasing the likelihood of a lawsuit. If you or a loved one is in a second marriage, make sure the estate planning is done and done right.

Is it worth the fight?

Chapter Eleven

Have you ever thought about how you would feel if your parent left everything to your siblings or a second spouse and left you with nothing?

No one likes to think of the possibility of being disinherited in favor of someone else… be they a brother or sister, second wife or husband, or even a "friend" or caregiver. When someone receives a greater share (or even the entire share) of an inheritance through a will or trust, the natural reaction of the remaining family members is usually shock, anger and outrage. But what can be done about it? Is the disinherited family member left out in the cold?

Not surprisingly, it depends. That's why the law allows for a "will (or trust) contest."

How ironic that a simple concept can spark such drama. Wills are intended to be uncomplicated. You leave instructions for how your property is to pass when you are gone. Trusts can (and should) be much more complex, yet at the heart they are nothing more than sophisticated instructions. So why do families frequently

Will and Trust Contests

A "will contest" or "trust contest" is a legal proceeding through which someone challenges the validity of a will or trust in court. The party asserting the challenge asks the judge or jury to rule that the document in question is invalid, based on certain legal standards. If they win, the court will turn to a prior estate plan or to the intestate laws of the state to decide who inherits the assets.

become so crazy over these simple directives? Sometimes the answer is complicated, but often it is as basic as the concept of the will itself: money... money... money!

"He received more than me!"

"She was cut out."

"It's not fair that I didn't get my share!"

This does not mean that money is the only driving force — far from it. It may be a longing for respect, feelings of rejection, abandonment, jealousy or anger... and even suspicion of wrongdoing. All of these emotions can drive will and trust contests. Sometimes it really does boil down to simple greed. It can be greed by the person who was cut out, or, in many cases, greed of the person who exploited a senior citizen into changing the will or trust.

Either way, when someone thinks about seeing a lawyer to challenge a will or trust, it's time to put the feelings to the side and get down to business. That's a big part of what attorneys are for in situations like this. Is there a valid basis to challenge the will or not? Should you even talk to a lawyer? If someone else started a will or trust contest against you, how do you go about defending yourself?

These questions are not easy, and there are a couple reasons why. Will and trust contests, like most types of litigation, are usually expensive. But they also have an added cost... they can tear families apart. Of course, many times the families are already broken before any lawyers get involved. A will may serve as a final passive-aggressive move to achieve revenge, or a fair and equal sounding trust may perturb a loved one who feels they deserved more than others.

Whatever the situation, court battles over wills or trusts should never be entered into lightly. They are too expensive financially and emotionally. For example, many crafty estate planning attorneys like to use "No Contest Clauses," sometimes referred to as "Terror Clauses." Remember the Frank Sinatra will which is widely cited as a famous example of one of these clauses.

These can be a handy way to dissuade a challenge. If someone who would otherwise be cut out of a will or trust gets something of value, he or she must think long and hard about the possibility of losing what they have to fight for more. In many states, these clauses are not upheld in wills, at least where the person bringing the challenge has a good faith reason to do so. These states believe that people should be free to pursue their legal rights in court without fear of reprisal. However, in some states, even when these provisions are not valid in wills, they may still be allowed if they appear in a trust. Anyone wanting to challenge a will or trust should think carefully if there is a No Contest Clause, depending on the state.

Even without that provision, will and trust contests are serious business. In cases where there is enough money and a good reason to fight, then will and trust contests serve an important role. Many times, the legacy of the one who passed deserves to be protected by fighting to honor the person's actual wishes. This is especially true when someone took advantage of a weakened mental or physical condition to coerce a new will or trust. Other times, the only things accomplished are broken families and handsomely paid attorneys.

the TRUE STORY
of ASIA'S RICHEST WOMAN!

Nina Wang was Asia's richest woman and one of the wealthiest women in the world. Always an eccentric woman (she frequently wore twin pony tails and mini-skirts even into her 60's), and once boasted she could live off of $400 per month. She died of cancer, without children, on April 3, 2007. Her fortune was estimated to be as high as $13 billion (in US dollars). So who inherited this vast wealth? Her feng shui master, of course.

Tony Chan was her personal consultant of all things feng shui. Feng shui is an ancient Chinese philosophy that is used to balance the energies in spaces people occupy to promote good health and fortune. (But you already knew that, right?) It must be pretty powerful stuff because Nina Wang signed a will in 2006 leaving the esteemed Tony Chan everything.

This will replaced a prior will from four years earlier that benefited charity and family members. So of course, the 2006 will was promptly attacked in court, launching perhaps the biggest will contest proceeding Asia has ever seen. They claimed that Chan used undue influence by convincing Wang that she would enjoy eternal life (or at least a very, very long life) by signing the will. Sadly, it didn't work — she was 69 when she passed.

Chan fired back. There was no fraud or trickery at all, his probate attorney argued; he was Nina Wang's secret lover! For 14 years, Chan said, she would sneak off to meet him for midnight meetings as far back as 1993. They covered their tracks by saying she was going for feng shui consultations, but it was really all about the love.

The case became even more interesting when the lawyers again appeared in court. At a preliminary court hearing, lawyers gave the judge a report by another feng shui master that stated Chan had tricked Wang into signing the will by telling her it would be used in a feng shui ceremony in which it would be burned. Chan instead secretly kept the will, pulling it out in 2007 after Wang died. Chan of course denied it.

The trial lasted for more than four months. A few new details came to light. First, the charity's probate attorney contended that the recent will was a forgery, and that Nina Wang was too ill from cancer to sign her name in 2006. Second, the feng shui master who claimed Nina Wang left all her money to him out of love was married during their secret love affair.

Finally, the charity's lawyer pointed out that the feng shui master received millions of dollars from Wang already, during her life, as payment for the advice he gave her.

The real irony of the case is that Nina Wang herself gained her vast fortune from... oh yes, a successful will contest case! Her husband was kidnapped in 1990 and eventually declared dead. In the meantime, she turned his company into a multi-billion dollar empire.

Her elderly father-in-law challenged her in court, saying in 2002 that Wang's husband wrote her out of his will when he learned she had an affair in the 1960s. Wang lost the case, and even the appellate judges ruled against her, declaring the will that left her everything was a forgery. Wang was criminally charged with forging her husband's will.

The highest appellate court in Hong Kong disagreed and ruled in Nina Wang's favor. The judges who upheld the will in Wang's favor awarded her husband's fortune to her. The criminal charges of forgery were dropped.

At the time this edition went to print, the Hong Kong judge had not yet ruled whether the feng shui master was as lucky as Wang had been when she was alive and fighting for the fortune. So make sure to check in with TrialAndHeirs.com to see how this exciting case comes out!

Did a loved one die with a will or trust that says something which you know wasn't what he or she really wanted?

Avoid a family fight!

A will contest is the classic example of a probate family fight. Was the document valid? Did it really express the decedent's intent? Was he or she competent, tricked, or confused? Or was he or she fully aware of what was signed? Was a lawyer involved, or was it a do-it-yourself special? And just what do the decedent's doctors, friends, neighbors and mailman have to say?

These are what will and trust contest cases are all about. If you find yourself facing a possible will contest — or if you are thinking about starting one — talk to an experienced probate litigation attorney as soon as possible. Accept no substitutes; talk to an attorney who specializes in cases of this nature. How can you tell if a lawyer really is a pro at probate litigation or not? Read on; by the end of this section, you'll likely know more than most attorneys who don't specialize in this area.

Chapter Twelve

To know whether or not a will or trust contest is worth the fight, you must first understand the basics of the law. The first step is to examine the "formalities."

There are a few requirements for the formalities of a will, and they vary from state to state. But to boil it down to simple terms, there are a few basic questions to ask: Did the person who created it properly sign it? Have two witnesses signed it to "attest" to the will's validity? Does it set forth the decedent's final wishes about his property?

In most states that is all you need. There are a few very technical exceptions that rarely occur and can't be explained without a detailed legal treatise. (And we wouldn't want to bore you with them here.)

What kind of formalities?

The "formalities" of a will or trust is a legal requirement that examines, essentially, whether the 'I's are dotted and 'T's are crossed. Or literally, can you tell if the document meets the legal standards for a valid will or trust by reading it? In other words, does the will or trust appear legally proper?

Setting those aside, the keys are that the person must have written down his or her wishes that the document dispose of the property after death, indicate to whom the property passes, be signed by the will's creator (usually at or near the end) and be signed by two witnesses who can vouch for the decedent's signature and wishes.

Some states vary this slightly by allowing one witness who is a notary to substitute for two witnesses.

Laws on the validity of trusts vary more throughout the country, but for the most part, they mirror the requirements of a will. In many states, a trust can even be oral (at least when no real estate is involved). But putting the rare verbal trusts aside, the document must show the testator's intent and his or her wishes for disposing of property, be signed, and sometimes witness signatures are also required. A trust has the additional requirement of naming a trustee. (Remember? That's the person who will administer the trust.) Doesn't sound too complicated, does it?

In the large majority of cases, it's not. But there are exceptions. For example, the witness part is often easy. Was the will or trust signed by two people of at least 18 years of age who were competent, and who did not receive anything through the will? If not, the will is invalid, except in some states that allow even beneficiaries to be witnesses. When a will is prepared by an estate planning attorney, usually he or she supplies the witnesses (such as the attorney and a legal assistant).

When someone tries to prepare a will by himself, the witness component can become more interesting. Did the witnesses really see the testator sign the will? Were they aware that the person was signing a will, rather than some other document? Can the witness really "attest" or verify that the person had the intent and the capacity to create a last will and testament? These are important questions. A witness must be able to verify this intent (at least in most states). In about half the states, the witness requirement can be skipped altogether if the entire document is written in the testator's own handwriting.

As discussed in Chapter Three, this is called a "holographic will." Remember the case about the farmer who scratched his wishes into a tractor bumper? No one witnessed that "will," but it was found valid. Holographic wills, like the farmer's bumper, can be valid even without any witnesses in states that allow them.

The signing part also appears simple, but this can be missed when someone prepares a will without an attorney. And what happens when the person signing isn't capable of providing a full signature? In most states, an "X" or other mark can suffice under the right conditions if the person intended it to be a valid will and wasn't capable of signing a full name. Of course, this may open a new host of questions, such as: was the person really competent if she couldn't sign her own name? And don't forget about a classic source of will disputes — the forgery. Most will contest lawyers know multiple handwriting experts just in case the question arises.

These experts can usually tell, by comparing the signature on the will to other examples from the same time frame, whether the decedent actually signed it. A forged signature means the will is not valid. Remember the classic case of Howard Hughes (from Chapter Four) that turned on this very issue. In most cases, there is no question that a will or trust appears valid. It is rare to have a valid objection based on a signature, date or the witnesses. Instead, when there is a question of a will's validity on its face, it usually turns on an ambiguity or mistake inside the document.

In other words, a will or trust can meet all the technical requirements but spark a challenge based on something vague or contradictory. What if the document isn't clear about its purpose? What if the same property is left to multiple people without explanation, or what if some property is forgotten altogether? And what happens when there was an obvious mistake but the intent was clear? A court proceeding is the only way to clear up problems like these. And the results can sometimes be surprising.

the TRUE STORY
of THE MARITAL MIX-UP!

New York residents Harvey and Rose Snide wanted to take care of their affairs the right way. They hired an attorney and created identical wills to leave their estates to one another, and then on to their children. On August 13, 1970, their attorney held an execution ceremony during which he presented Harvey and Rose their wills in envelopes bearing their respective names. They dutifully removed the wills and signed them, as did the attesting witnesses. The documents, as prepared, met all of the proper formalities to qualify as valid wills.

There was only one problem. No one bothered to read the wills during the execution ceremony. Not Harvey and not Rose. Not the witnesses. And not the attorney. They all missed one very important aspect that was not discovered until after Harvey took his last breath.

Harvey and Rose's wills had accidentally been placed into the wrong envelopes. Harvey signed the will written for Rose, and Rose the one for Harvey. Instead of leaving their estates to each other, the will Harvey signed technically left everything to him.

The matter was brought to court (because, remember, all wills must pass through probate court to be effective). At first, everyone agreed that the wills should be substituted because that was what Harvey and Rose intended. But one of their three children was a minor. The child could not legally consent, so the court appointed an attorney — called a "Guardian ad Litem" — to protect the child's interests and make the decision on the child's behalf.

The Guardian ad Litem, named David Johnson, had a problem. His legal duty was to the child and the child alone. Technically, if the will was rejected as invalid, the child would inherit some of Harvey's estate due to New York's intestacy laws. If the will was honored, everything would go to Rose.

So David Johnson objected. He argued that the will did not meet the test of formalities. Once courts started reading "intent" into a will, when would it stop? This case may seem clear, but what about the next one, and the one after that? Only with a clear rule can this problem be avoided.

The judge disagreed and chose to honor the will and Harvey's intent. David Johnson appealed to the Appellate Division of the Supreme Court. The judges who reviewed the case agreed with Johnson. They reversed the judge and threw out the will.

Rose Snide's attorney then appealed that decision to the highest court in New York. Seven judges reviewed the case this time. After careful deliberation, on February 19, 1981, four of the seven ruled that Harvey's intent should be followed. The other three disagreed. But four out of seven did the trick, and Rose Snide won.

Sounds like basic common sense, right? Everyone knows what Harvey intended and it was just as a simple mistake. Why not honor his wishes? The three judges who disagreed believed that they were required by law to focus on the "paper writing itself." Because Harvey did not intend the paper he signed to be his last will and testament, these three judges believed it could not survive the test of formalities.

These three judges were not alone. The exact same situation also came to the attention of a probate court in Allegheny County, Pennsylvania. In that case, the probate court, the first appellate court and even the Supreme Court of Pennsylvania all rejected the will. Unlike the New York judges, the ones in Pennsylvania felt that the law would have no meaning if it was disregarded to do "equity and justice." They followed the law of formalities to the letter and were not swayed by what the husband and wife really intended.

Which was the right result? It depends on whom you ask. But one thing is clear, after the Harvey and Rose Snide case, their attorney likely read every will he prepared twice during the execution ceremony.

Have you really read your will or trust?

Avoid a family fight!

You would think it is obvious, but apparently not. Read your will and trust before you sign. Every word of the will, and the important parts of the trust (at least). Do not rely on your attorney with blind faith. Of course, you should rightly trust your attorney, but even the best attorneys have been known to make mistakes. This is your legacy on the line; make sure everything is right. At the very least, take home your will or trust and read it after you sign it, but before you file it away for safekeeping. A new document can always be prepared if you find a mistake. If you fail to do this, and the mistake is found after you pass, it may be too late. At the very least, you expose your heirs to costly court proceedings that could have been avoided.

Mom wasn't in her right mind

Chapter Thirteen

Nearly every good will or trust contest has a key question in dispute: Was the person who signed the will or trust competent when it was signed? In other words, did he or she have sufficient legal capacity to execute a valid will or trust?

What exactly does this mean? For wills, the test is one of "testamentary" capacity. For most states, the issue is broken down into three separate parts. Did the testator (the will's creator): (1) know the natural objects of his or her bounty, (2) have the ability to recall the nature and extent of his or her property, and (3) have the capacity to make a rational plan for disposing of his or her property?

What is testamentary capacity?

"Testamentary capacity" is a legal test of whether the person who signed the will or trust was mentally capable of sufficiently understanding it.

That sure cleared things up for you, right? Don't get overwhelmed; it's really not complicated. Let's take it one by one.

First, what is the "natural object" of one's "bounty?" (And, no, we're not talking about the paper towels.) This means whether the testator knew his family members to whom he would ordinarily leave his property. Or even more simply, did Grandma know all of her kids and grandkids? If the answer is yes, then this part of the test is probably met.

The second part is knowing the nature and extent of one's property. This is fairly self evident, but can be trickier than one might think at first blush. Is it sufficient to know you have investments, but not know where or how much? Do you have to know how much your property is worth? What if you forgot you had something, like some stock that was in your possession for years but you never really thought about it?

For the most part, courts do not expect the testator to memorize and remember every last detail about their property. If the person has the ability to recall what he or she owns, that is likely sufficient. It depends on the person, of course. If the decedent was a sophisticated stockbroker but could not recall whether or not he had mutual funds, this may signal that he can no longer meet this part of the test. If the testator (in contrast) never really was good with investments, perhaps because his or her spouse took care of the finances, then having a general knowledge that there are investments somewhere is likely enough. Clearly, the person cannot be expected to understand more than he or she would have earlier in life.

The final part is often the most difficult one. Is the person able to create and understand a rational plan to dispose of property? If the will leaves everything to the man in the moon, there is an easy answer. But what happens if the decedent's will directs that one child is cut out in favor of another? Was the person disinherited due to a rational choice by a sound mind, or was it due to advanced age, infirmity or disability? This is where the cases get tricky.

Before we explore this in more detail, you may be asking — what about a trust? Why spend so much time discussing the standard of a will, if trusts are so darn important?

States look at most trusts in one of two ways. First, remember that there are two types of trusts. Most trusts are "living" trusts. These trusts, discussed in Section II, come into being before death. The other, less common type is the "testamentary trust," which is created by the will and comes into existence after death. Because these testamentary trusts are created through wills, courts use the exact same competency test as they do for a will.

For living trusts, most states treat them a little differently. There are states that treat living trusts under the same standard as a will because they serve a very similar purpose. The majority view, however, is that a living trust is treated like a contract. The test, generally speaking (again, many states use different words), is whether the person who created it reasonably comprehended what he or she was doing. Sort of vague, isn't it?

Either for trusts, or wills, the test turns on that key question of whether the person really understood what he was signing. This crucial inquiry depends largely on the facts of each individual case.

And sometimes, there is more at stake than most people can fathom.

the TRUE STORY
of JOHNSON & JOHNSON!

One of the largest health care companies in the world began modestly in 1887, on the fourth floor of an old wallpaper factory. It started with a simple concept — saving lives through sterilization. As the doctors discovered the role that germs played on people's health, Johnson & Johnson was there to help with sterilized bandages. It introduced to the world its patented baby powder, dental floss, first aid kits, sanitary napkins and of course, Band-Aids.

The company grew phenomenally well into 250 companies based in 60 different countries. Until the early 2000's, Company revenues grew 71 years in a row, reaching more than $47 billion. The Johnson family enjoyed a great deal of wealth, to say the least. By the 1980s, J. Steward Johnson was the heir to the Johnson & Johnson fortune. He was a noted hypochondriac and had little interest in business.

His six children reported his shortcomings as a father, including neglect, abuse and even incest. Johnson died of cancer on May 23, 1983 at the age of 87. His estate was worth $500 million. At the time, it was reported to be one of the largest ever to pass through New York's Surrogate Court (again, that's what probate court is called in New York).

Johnson's last will and testament was dated April 14, 1983 — just weeks before his death. In it, he left everything to his third wife of 12 years who was 42 years younger than he was. That's almost in Anna Nicole Smith territory (stay tuned for that one!) Barbara "Basia" Piasecka was a Polish-born immigrant who joined the Johnson household as a chambermaid. The six children — all from prior marriages — filed suit and the case dragged on for two years until reaching trial. An oceanic charitable foundation, which faced a reduced bequest under the new will, joined the children in the fight.

With the help of 210 lawyers, 22 law firms, and $24 million in legal fees, the trial lasted four months and produced 15,000 pages of sworn testimony. The case centered on one question: Was Johnson mentally competent when he signed the final will? His children were already well-to-do from lifetime trusts that helped them accumulate combined wealth of nearly half a billion dollars. They called to the stand 37 witnesses who claimed that their late father was anything but capable of understanding his final will. These witnesses testified he was disoriented and even hallucinated during the time in question.

Some people told about incidents of name calling and even physical abuse that Mrs. Johnson inflicted on him. Mrs. Johnson called 38 witness of her own (not wanting to be outdone). They, of course, believed Johnson to be sharp and alert until his dying day. His personal masseur testified how coherent he was during his final months and how close he was to his wife. The widow's attorneys also pointed out that Johnson had created dozens of wills and other estate planning documents which also excluded the children, because he felt he had given them enough already through their living trusts.

The trial became so intense and heated that, at one point, fifteen workers who supported the widow began shouting "liar" and "communist." Court bailiffs and attorneys scattered through the crowd trying to restore order during the ensuing pandemonium. (Now that would have been a fun trial to sit through!) The presiding judge sentenced the "leader" of the group to two weeks in jail and imposed fines on many of the rest. The judge was rewarded with at least three telephone death threats.

After four months of well-publicized dramatics, the attorneys for the warring factions presented their closing arguments. Jurors who were interviewed later testified that they supported the children and found the testimony of the attorney who prepared the final will to be less than helpful to the widow's cause.

Interestingly, this attorney, Nina Zagat, stood to earn more than $10 million in fees for serving as executor and trustee through the final estate planning documents. After hearing the medical experts hired by Mrs. Johnson, jurors believed J. Steward had been "disturbed." Yet the jury never had the chance to issue a verdict.

After a series of all-night negotiating sessions, the parties reached a settlement. Of the $500 million, $80 million went for taxes, almost $50 million were for the children (plus another $10 million for their legal fees), $20 million to the charity, and the former chambermaid kept more than $300 million. She certainly must have been good at her job to catch the eye (and ultimately the wallet) of Johnson. There was no word on how many Band-Aids she was allowed to keep.

Are you worried that someone may challenge a will or trust that is being prepared?

Avoid a family fight!

In nearly every heated will contest, doctors and other medical experts stand at the center of the dispute. If you are worried someone may start a court fight over a will or trust, suggest that the testator be evaluated by a qualified doctor as close to the day of signing as possible. It also helps if the attorney who prepared the document is well-credentialed and truly independent. An attorney who stands to gain from the will or trust, through later legal fees, will not make a very compelling witness if the will is challenged in court. Certainly Mrs. Johnson could have gained much if these lessons were followed. Of course, one could argue that if more reputable doctors and attorneys were involved when the will was signed, Mr. Johnson might never have been allowed to sign it in the first place.

The TRUE STORY
of BROOKE ASTOR!

The eyes of New York — and much of the rest of the world — closely watched the trial over Brooke Astor's last wishes. But, unlike most legal contests about whether a will was valid, this one had much more at stake than who would inherit Brooke Astor's millions.

Her son, Anthony Marshall, and her former lawyer were criminally charged with forgery, fraud, grand larceny, possession of stolen property and falsifying business records, among other crimes. Prosecutors alleged that they conspired to convince Astor to change her will to redirect some $60 million from charities to her only son Marshall when she was incompetent. They also claimed Marshall stole and sold a painting worth tens of millions, used his mother's money to pay for cleaning his yacht and taking care of his own property, paid himself millions in salary for helping his mother, and otherwise took advantage of her declining mental state.

Brooke Astor was considered the Queen of New York society until she died at the age of 105 on August 13, 2007. She left behind an estate and trust with a combined value estimated at almost $200 million, even after devoting much of her life to charity. In a New York Times article written by Marilyn Berger on August 13, 2007, it was noted that Astor's motto was "Money is like manure; it's not worth a thing unless it's spread around." The same article refers to Astor as the First Lady of Philanthropy.

It was no surprise that her last will (number 31 in her lifetime) in 2002 left much of her vast wealth to charity. But prosecutors were more interested in the codicils to her will that began in December 2003. As you may recall from chapter four, a codicil is simply an amendment to a will. It is because of their interest and the extraordinary amount of money at stake, that the Brooke Astor trial serves as one of the most unusual will contest cases in history.

So why did the prosecutors suspect criminal wrongdoing regarding the codicils to the will? For starters, Brooke Astor was diagnosed with Alzheimer's disease back in 2000, And Marshall himself wrote a letter to her doctor in December of 2000 detailing Astor's symptoms of the disease.

Yet, prosecutors did not challenge the first codicil of December 2003, or any documents that came before. They focused on the codicils that followed. They likely were less concerned about the prior documents because the $60 million in dispute still went to charity under those wills and trusts.

As of that time, Marshall was to receive seven percent interest, per year, from the $60 million, and charities would receive what was left when he died. With prudent investing, this meant the entire $60 million could have remained, even with the substantial yearly distributions to Marshall. Prosecutors contended that Marshall wanted more.

While he was already wealthy and estranged from his children, the 85-year old Marshall reportedly wanted someone else to benefit after he passed. Namely, he wanted to benefit his wife, Charlene, who was 20 years younger than Marshall. Astor had made significant changes in her estate planning documents in prior years to make sure that Charlene did not inherit her wealth (even Marshall's lawyers admitted that Astor did not like Charlene).

Prosecutors alleged that Marshall and his co-conspirator, lawyer Francis X. Morrissey, Jr., schemed to coerce Astor to change her will so that Marshall could control the $60 million and pass it along to Charlene when he died. The pair arranged for a different estate planning attorney to prepare a new codicil to the will.

On January 12, 2004, Astor signed the second codicil, which gave Marshall the authority to leave all of the $60 million to whomever he wanted when he passed, instead of to charity. In other words, this meant Charlene. The second codicil also replaced Astor's prior lawyer as her executor and named Morrissey in his place. This change meant future fees worth millions for Morrissey.

Apparently, the pair still wasn't satisfied. In March 2004, a third codicil was signed that directed all of Astor's real estate to be sold and added to the $60 million pot at her death. Only Morrissey and two assistants were present when Astor signed this document.

Or did she? Prosecutors claimed that she never signed it and relied on expert testimony that her signature was forged.

Although will contest cases like this one are common in probate and other civil courts around the country, it is very rare for one to occur in a criminal court. Why? Cases challenging the validity of a will, trust or codicil are hard to prove without very compelling evidence. Plus the burden of proof in criminal court is much higher than in a traditional lawsuit or probate proceeding where money — not someone's freedom — is at stake. "Beyond a reasonable doubt" applies in criminal court, but not in probate or civil proceedings.

Further, prosecutors seldom have the time, resources, or inclination to try to put together a case of fraud, forgery or similar claims for a will contest case. For them to do so in this case, and commit themselves to a trial lasting months (in total it lasted almost six months), they must have been very confident in the case.

Of course, they did have powerful evidence on their side (including Astor's Alzheimer's diagnosis and Marshall's letter about her condition from 2000). They also called dozens of witnesses who testified, to varying degrees, that Astor was not mentally competent during the time in question. Plus, it was also very odd that the second and third codicils were done in such a relaxed manner, considering they controlled tens of millions of dollars.

Despite this evidence, the prosecutors still had a difficult task. They weren't present when Astor signed the will codicils. Neither were the judge or jurors. The large majority of the witnesses who testified at trial weren't there either.

The law focuses on Astor's mental state at the moment she signed the codicils. Not the days (or even hours) before or after. Why? Older people with declining mental abilities usually have both good and bad days. But the bad times don't count if the person was mentally clear and aware of what she was signing when she put pen to paper.

Yet the prosecution spent six months trying to prove, beyond a reasonable doubt, that Astor was wasn't competent to sign the codicils, and her 85-year old son should be sent to jail because of it.

So what happened? The jury found Marshall guilty of 14 of the 16 counts, including the charges that he committed fraud in convincing his mother to change her will. He faces up to 25 years in jail. Of course, at age 85, there is a question of how much time he'll actually serve. Plus, his attorneys have already promised to appeal.

Be sure to check in at TrialAndHeirs.com to see how he fares on appeal, as well as in the upcoming will contest case (in probate court) that will decide how much of his inheritance he'll be allowed to keep.

What do you think could have been done to avoid this costly legal battle?

Avoid a family fight!

When drastic estate planning changes are done with someone elderly, especially one who has already been diagnosed with Alzheimer's disease, any good estate planning lawyer would only allow the document to be signed with substantial evidence that the person was competent at the time of the execution. At the very least, this means the lawyer must thoroughly question the person, including what is commonly known as a "mini-mental evaluation." This probes a person's knowledge of things such as the date, time and place, the name of the president, and many questions of memory and comprehension that most adults could easily answer.

In even more questionable cases with substantial dollars on the line, a good estate planning attorney would go the extra mile of having a doctor evaluate the person on or near the date of signing. Ideally, they would also videotape the meeting when the will or codicil was executed to prove that the person knew what he or she was signing (at least when a legal challenge could be expected). The extensive coverage of the Astor case by the New York media makes no mention of any of this being done.

Why wasn't this done when Brooke Astor signed those questionable codicils to her will? If they had, either she wouldn't have been permitted to sign the documents, or her son could have easily documented her competent mind and likely avoided the entire trial.

How does this work in the real world?

Chapter Fourteen

We know... cases about mental competency seem pretty complicated. Six month trials and millions upon millions of dollars spent on legal fees. How can the non-lawyers of the world understand them? Don't worry! When you break this down to simpler concepts, it's not really that hard.

Legal work isn't always as complicated as the legal tests make it seem. You don't need to take a bar exam to understand how will contest cases work. When you boil it all down to its essence, the legal question of mental competence turns on whether the person was of sound mind and understood what he or she signed. In the end, common sense usually prevails.

But that still doesn't tell us how an attack on a will or trust based on lack of capacity works in the real world. There are several important factors to keep in mind.

First, as we explored in the Brooke Astor case, the test is based on when the document was signed. Many people suffer the terrible effects of Alzheimer's disease or dementia. Recent estimates place those diagnosed with Alzheimer's at more than five million in this country, with a new person labeled with this disease every 72 seconds.

People who are diagnosed with mild or often even moderate dementia or Alzheimer's disease have good days and bad — and even positive moments and negative ones in the same day. Some people are good in the morning, but very confused in the afternoon. Many are very aware and coherent one day, but very forgetful and confused the next.

This reality makes attacking a will or trust based on lack of capacity very difficult. Except in rare cases, the challenger was not present when it was signed, and the only people who were — the attorney and witnesses — will likely support the validity of the will or trust. Otherwise, they would not have signed it in the first place.

So what do you do if you find yourself reading a will or trust document that you don't think is right because the person was not competent? There are three good sources. The first, and most important, is medical records. If the medical records do not support any basis for confusion, memory loss or other signs of mental decline, then chances are that a will contest on this ground will be very difficult, if not impossible. Of course, talking to the physicians themselves instead of just relying on the medical records can be more helpful, particularly in the case of a doctor who has seen the testator many times. Nurses, caregivers and other healthcare professionals are also helpful because of their medical training and experience.

The second source is witness testimony... and this doesn't mean you and your spouse. Obviously, everyone who wants to challenge a will or trust because they were cut out may feel that the person was not competent, while the person supporting the validity of the document will say the opposite. Testimony of those involved, and their spouses, can be very important, but independent people — those who do not stand to benefit in any way — are usually even more critical. The potential witnesses who can help include friends, relatives (brothers, sisters, cousins), and others who came into contact with the decedent on a regular basis around the time in question. This is why the Johnson and Brooke Astor trials took so long... many, many witnesses testified about the mental state of each of them.

The final source is other evidence of irrational actions, or a pattern of actions and inactions, which demonstrate the lack of a competent mind. For example, did the person stop paying bills? Did he or she need help getting dressed everyday? Was the person able to make investment decisions, remember birthdays, or have intelligent conversations about politics or their own medical affairs? Was there a last-minute change in the will or trust that varied from prior documents, and if so, what was the reason for it? These are all factors that can help decide a will or trust contest case, especially when there are irrefutable documents that shed light on these questions.

In general, the person challenging a will or trust based on lack of proper mental capacity has the uphill battle. Most states recognize a presumption of validity — in other words, the party bringing the claim has the burden of proving lack of capacity. Plus, when witnesses and an attorney are involved, you have to deal with seemingly independent witnesses who were there at the moment of signing. Because the attorney and supporting witnesses literally put their name on the line for that will or trust, of course they will testify that they believed the person was competent when it was signed. And the attorney has more assumed credibility because his or her career is also on the line.

Additionally, to win a will or trust contest based on lack of capacity, you need to have an expert testify for you, unless the facts and records are clearly in your favor (and even then, you may still want one.) Expert witnesses are paid medical experts who can testify from experience and education — after reviewing the medical records and other evidence — whether the person was mentally capable of understanding what he or she signed. These experts are usually not cheap and can always be attacked by an expert on the other side who says exactly the opposite. Sometimes it seems like attorneys can find a paid expert to testify to almost anything.

The key to these tricky cases is to have an experienced attorney in your corner. No one should be left to figure things out without help. If you are faced with such a situation, either as the attacker or the defender, talk to a qualified attorney and see what your options are. Often times, you may have more options than you realize.

the TRUE STORY
of LEONA HELMSLEY!

She was known to all as the "Queen of Mean." Leona Helmsley became famous in the late 1980s when she was charged with — and found guilty of — tax evasion. She reportedly felt that "only the little people pay taxes." Of course, most "little people" don't spend 19 months in federal prison, as she did. Her tax troubles did not stop her from passing away with assets reportedly worth $4 to $8 billion. She died on August 20, 2007, at the age of 87, from congestive heart failure.

Yes, this does prove that she had a heart after all. In fact, she left most of her wealth to charity, through charitable trusts she and her late husband had created. But the money was earmarked primarily to benefit dogs, not people. Helmsley had four grandchildren; her only child was a son who died years before she did. She also left behind Trouble, a well-named Maltese. To care for her dog, Helmsley created a $12 million dollar trust for Trouble alone. As you can imagine, this definitely resulted in a lot of "trouble!"

In stark contrast, two of her four grandchildren were left nothing "for reasons that are known to them" as spelled out in the will. According to reports, the reason for this was that the two grandchildren did not name any of their children after her late husband. She did leave the other two grandchildren $10 million each, but only on the condition they visit her grave at least yearly.

Faced with these glaring inequities, Helmsley's two excluded grandchildren filed a lawsuit, claiming that she was not mentally fit or competent to create the will and trust. The judge assigned to the case also addressed whether Trouble really needed all 12 million big ones.

Only seven months after she passed, Helmsley's estate and the two excluded heirs settled for a tidy sum of $6 million, tax-free, plus payment of all their legal fees. Not a bad result. In fact, they ended up doing better than the dog. Trouble found his inheritance of $12 million slashed to a paltry $2 million. The judge ruled this was more than enough to pay for Trouble's yearly expenses, including a full-time security detail, a well-paid guardian, and all the grooming and gourmet food a spoiled Maltese named Trouble could want.

While Trouble's $10 million loss was spent in large part on settling with the two grandchildren, at least the deal provided Trouble with some peace of mind. The settlement resolved the will contest and also bought the grandchildren's silence. That way, Trouble's final days would not be interrupted by Helmsley's grandchildren telling negative stories to the media about their late grandmother.

Are you involved in a will or trust contest case?

Avoid a family fight!

If you find yourself in the middle of a will or trust contest, consider a settlement before the feud reaches absurd costs. Few estates can afford a fight as complex as the one over the Johnson & Johnson legacy. There is no point in fighting over a modest estate if most of the estate value is eaten up in legal fees. Leona Helmsley's grandchildren and executors realized this and saved everyone involved a great deal of aggravation and money.

Of course, it does take two to tango. If one side is unwilling to find a reasonable middle-ground, then the other side has no option left but to go forward and fight or give up. The emotions involved seldom allow someone to walk away with nothing. And in Leona Helmsley's case, every dog should have its day.

Undue influence — abusing the trust

Chapter Fifteen

Now this sounds pretty cool — "undue influence." What a great way to attack a will or trust you don't like. But, what is it? How can "influence" be "undue?"

Undue influence occurs when people abuse the confidence and trust placed in them. It is usually done to convince someone to name them as a beneficiary of some or all of the property, when the person really didn't want to do so. The classic example is an attorney convincing a client to name him or her as a beneficiary in a will or trust. Heaven forbid — an attorney! Doing something that underhanded?

Yes, it happens. In fact, many states specifically prevent an attorney from preparing a will and being named as a beneficiary in it (with certain exceptions). A client goes to an attorney and places trust and confidence in him or her to prepare a proper estate plan. If the attorney uses this trust and confidence to benefit financially from the will or trust , there is a strong likelihood of undue influence (and no, charging legal fees for creating the document, or even serving as executor or trustee, doesn't count).

Think about it — who goes to an attorney

> **Undue Influence**
>
> *"Undue Influence" is a legal challenge to a will, trust or other method of passing title to an asset (such as changing the title to a bank account or house, or even making a gift). This legal doctrine focuses on whether someone used coercion, deceit, force or trickery to compel the decedent to do or sign something that he or she wouldn't have otherwise done.*

for a will and ends up leaving property to the attorney through the will? It sure would be fishy in most cases. Like almost every other area in the law, the issue of undue influence is typically not so black and white. While a key component of undue influence is trust and confidence, the crucial question is whether that trust and confidence was abused. People can — and should — reward those whom they trust and confide in for help. So how do you know if improper coercion or similar behavior was involved?

Every state has a test for it, and the factors for this test do vary from state to state. But the key components are whether the person was susceptible to improper influence and whether the influence used actually changed the mind of the person. The influence must also be "undue" — meaning inappropriate or excessive in some way. Simply asking for a gift or will bequest is not generally enough. Moral or physical coercion, intimidation, scare tactics, excessive flattery, and threats to withhold love or support are all examples of influence that go beyond the boundaries of acceptable and instead become undue, depending on the severity.

Another important question to ask is whether the bequest was different from the natural expectation. In other words, if someone leaves all her money to her children equally, which is what one would expect, it would be a pretty hard case to prove that something undue happened. In fact, some states require that an unnatural disposition occur. On the other hand, if someone cuts out his children in favor of a caregiver, red flags go up all over the place, and you can bet that probate attorneys and judges alike will suspect undue influence.

People raising undue influence challenges often have one more legal weapon in their arsenal. In many states, courts will presume that undue influence occurred if certain conditions are met, such as a trusting and confidential relationship, an opportunity to exert undue influence and an unnatural disposition favoring the person who was the trusted confidant. In other words, when there clearly is a level of trust and other circumstances that suggest undue influence might have occurred, the law assumes it did, at least at first.

How does this legal presumption work? Often, the assumption that there was undue influence doesn't mean much. It temporarily shifts the burden of proof from the person attacking the will or trust to the person defending it. But, these laws usually also provide that once the defending person comes up with evidence that it was legitimate, then the burden of proof shifts back to the attacking party. Okay, so we're getting pretty technical here... but essentially it can become a legal ping pong game.

Let's get back to how this works in the real world. The bottom line remains that there has to be some proof that undue influence occurred. In practice, these cases usually go hand in hand with competence challenges. As you would expect, the medical and other records at the time, as well as neutral witness testimony, are very important to prove or defend an undue influence case. If the decedent told his neighbor how much the girlfriend was pestering him about his will, it would be a good sign of undue influence.

On the other hand, if someone discusses with a friend how much she appreciated all the care that one daughter provided, and that she deserves a little something extra, the friend's testimony would work in favor of upholding the will or trust. It all comes down to the facts; just the facts, ma'am, nothing but the facts. And in these cases, those facts can sometimes be quite extraordinary.

the TRUE STORY
of THE OVERLY AMBITIOUS NURSE

"I gave you the best sex you ever had," Brenda wrote to Jim, her 74-year-old ex-husband and current boyfriend. "The only way I will accept your company, and if you want me to be monogamous with you, I want my name to be on all your assets like it was before without it being able to be revoked."

Yes, this actually happened. And — luckily — Jim kept this letter and others like it.

For example, there was the one that said: "If you really loved me you would make sure I was all set financially and you don't. So now I want my dues without excuses (big time, Jim)." There was also the one where she called him a "low-life, scum-bag, rotten-lying, stingy-bastard." Even better, she wrote: "Keep all your money and put it up your [expletive!]. Slime-bag. You'll never get your *BLEEP* up again."

And this woman said she loved him. She even said she would marry him.

Jim's "girlfriend" Brenda was eight years younger than he was. But more importantly, she was a nurse with access to Viagra-like medicine that she injected into him so she and Jim could have sexual intercourse.

When Jim had been more coherent, he had seen Brenda for what she was. He divorced her, after a brief marriage, in July 1996. But a few years later, Jim's mental faculties began to slip. His memory became poor and he was sometimes confused.

Jim did not reach the point of incompetence yet, but he certainly was susceptible to undue influence. Brenda saw her opportunity and went for it. Sex in exchange for money! Hmmm... there's a name for that profession, right?

Just after Brenda wrote the letters, Jim transferred almost all of his assets, including his home, to Brenda. He rewrote his will and left almost everything to her, to the exclusion of his two daughters from his first marriage. All of this was done in private, so his family didn't know about the changes. Wow... it must have been some sex!

But Jim still lived alone. He functioned. He dressed himself, paid his bills on time, and was in no apparent danger. So his daughters allowed their father's relationship with Brenda to continue, despite their obvious concerns. Dad, they felt, deserved to make his own choices. They thought, "If he found happiness with this woman, who are we to interfere?"

Unfortunately, they did not know what was going on behind closed doors. Eventually, their suspicions grew to the point where they could not sit back and wait any longer. Jim's daughters filed petitions in probate court and asked for Jim to be declared incompetent. They wanted to protect him and felt he passed the point of making rational decisions.

But Brenda did not give up easily. She convinced Jim to hire an attorney and fight. The attorney filed paperwork contesting the proceedings, arguing that Jim was fully competent. That's when Jim's daughters went to see co-author Andrew.

Guardians and Conservators

When someone lacks the ability to make suitable or informed decisions (due to age, infirmity or other reasons), family members or others who care about the person can file a petition in court asking for someone to be appointed as the decision maker. This person is called Guardian and/or Conservator (some states use one term, some use the other, and some use both). Usually the appointed person is a family member (but not always). The person over whom a Guardian/ Conservator is appointed loses the legal ability to make some or all of their decisions.

Andrew took the case and convinced the Judge to have Jim evaluated by an independent neurologist. The doctor tested Jim thoroughly and found he suffered from dementia and possible Alzheimer's disease. He reported that Jim was no longer competent to make his own decisions. Based on that and other evidence, the judge appointed Jim's daughters as his Guardian and Conservator.

With Andrew's help, Jim's daughters started a separate lawsuit to recover all of Jim's assets and to overturn the will. Brenda's letters to Jim were critical to the case. Brenda testified in a deposition, under oath, that she never asked Jim to give her anything. Then Andrew showed her the letters and revealed the truth. Brenda's attorney realized her case was done and convinced her to take a settlement. Jim's daughters recovered everything, except for a pickup truck and a small sum of cash they allowed Brenda to keep.

The problem was that, even though the letters were powerful evidence, suing Brenda still cost money. Andrew advised them to settle and give Brenda something, rather than spending more in legal fees by taking the case to trial.

Without the letters, proving what Brenda really did to Jim would have been difficult, because the medical records and the fact he lived by himself showed he was not necessarily incompetent when the asset transfers and new will were done. But with Brenda's true colors made plain as day by the letters, Andrew was able to expose the truth.

Once again Jim's daughters could sleep at night, knowing that Jim would have money to live on through his final days. His financial legacy was kept intact to pay for his care, and ultimately to pass to his children, rather than traded away for sex.

If you want to learn more about Guardians and Conservators, sign up at TrialAndHeirs.com for more information. For example, many people smartly use powers of attorney to avoid the need of court intervention that is required for Guardians and Conservators.

Are you worried that someone may be unduly influencing one of your elderly or incapacitated loved ones?

Avoid a family fight!

It is not easy to know when to interfere in an elderly or incapacitated parent's life. Being older does not mean that someone cannot find new love. However, when signs of memory loss or confusion begin to show, it is time to have a frank discussion with your loved one. You should investigate, ask questions and probe. Yes, you may have to be discrete about it, and some parents may stubbornly refuse any help. But at least you need to try.

If you see or hear something that gives you concern that financial abuse is occurring, or that a greedy gold-digger is out to change the will or trust, it's time to talk to an experienced attorney about your rights. If you consult with an independent legal expert who's seen it before, he or she can help you decide if it's time to intervene and how to do it. Don't wait until it's too late! Despite the best evidence in the world in your favor, your loved one will always be better off if you stop the new will or trust from being signed in the first place.

Ideas to Spark Family Discussion

The best way to make sure that your elderly parent or other loved one leaves a will or trust that accurately reflects his or her true wishes, before incompetence sets in or undue influence occurs, is to ask. In a "normal" situation, you may not need to ask about who should get what. Just knowing a proper will or trust was done may be enough. In not-so-normal situations, such as second marriages or where certain children might be excluded in favor of others, probing a little more is certainly justified.

If your loved one begins to show signs of dementia or Alzheimer's disease, such as forgetfulness, confusion, memory loss, difficulty making decisions or having normal conversations, then you may want to ask to see a copy of the will or trust. Tell them you want to make sure they've taken care of their estate planning. Suggest you would like them to show you where it is in case you ever need to find it.

If your attempts are met with resistance, try a different approach. Start the conversation by telling him or her that you've heard horror stories about legal fights in probate court. There are so many rich and famous families who make headlines with will and trust contests. Many of these are included in this book. Use these stories as ice-breakers to bring up the topic. Then you can transition by saying something like, "Mom, I don't want this to ever happen to our family."

No parent or grandparent would ever want their legacy to end up different than they intended. If you let them know it can happen without the proper planning, and why you have concerns about your family, that should be enough to open the dialogue. If not, it may be time to talk to an experienced attorney to see what options you have. Or you can try sitting down with Mom or Dad along with a trusted friend, or even a good therapist, who can help talk some sense into a stubborn loved one.

If you wait too long and your parent is no longer competent, then the person with authority under a Power of Attorney, or the acting Guardian or Conservator, should not hesitate to search and find the will and trust. People filling these important roles have a duty to safeguard the incompetent person's wishes, and they cannot do so without first learning what the wishes are. If the will or trust cannot be located, the legal authority granted through a proper Power of Attorney, or Guardianship/Conservatorship court documents, can be used to request a copy from the attorney who prepared them, if they know who he or she is. They can also be used to access safety deposit boxes at banks, where many people store their wills and trusts.

Don't wait until after death to find out that there is an unexpected problem. Prevention and frank conversation are always the best cure.

But what if that simply is not possible in your family and you find yourself in the middle of a will or trust contest? If that happens, you should reach out and talk to the other side. If you cannot talk directly, there are mediators and counselors able to help. Often times, experienced attorneys who know the importance of saving legal fees and emotional turmoil will actually help facilitate a settlement. Not all attorneys are out to generate fees at the cost of their clients' needs (although it does happen, unfortunately). It is rare that anyone wins when a will or trust contest proceeds all the way to trial. It is almost always better — financially and emotionally — to find a middle ground and settle.

If not, then you will need a good attorney on your side to fight. The sooner you have an experienced attorney in your corner, the more options you have to resolve the case favorably.

SECTION IV

ASSET DISPUTES — BUT THEY WANTED ME TO HAVE IT!

Not only "where there's a will, there's a way," but actually more than one way! While using wills and trusts are the best way, some people try to **outsmart the probate system.**

When these same people don't want to pay for a trust, they use a shortcut. They add someone else's name to their bank accounts, deed to their house, or other assets. Or they may make gifts, without putting anything in writing. These inheritance shortcuts often lead to family fighting or even bigger problems.

In Chapter Sixteen you'll learn about JOINT OWNERSHIP — THE GOOD, THE BAD, AND THE UGLY. You'll discover the pitfalls that often occur. In fact, this shortcut can even cause someone to lose the very asset which he or she was trying to keep out of probate court.

"THE WILL AND TRUST CONTROL EVERYTHING, RIGHT?" You may wonder. Chapter Seventeen teaches that having a will and/or trust is not enough. Too many people undermine their own estate plans by contradicting them. You'll see how this can lead to a court fight. Even Princess Diana broke this rule and caused confusion and resentment.

Remember the famous Saturday Night Live sketch where

Dana Carvey played the Church Lady and said, "HOW CONVEEEENIENT!" Chapter Eighteen explores how this phrase takes on a whole new meaning when addressing issues of joint tenancy. A classic example occurred in Florida, where a multi-millionaire was killed by his girlfriend.

After someone dies, many people exclaim, "HURRAY! MY NAME IS ON THE LIFE INSURANCE." Chapter Nineteen tackles what can be an equally challenging issue. When people don't properly use life insurance in tandem with a trust, it can lead to family feuds. Whitney Houston knows this better than anyone.

Chapter Twenty delves into a hot-button issue for many families who say, "IT WAS A GIFT — REALLY." When someone claims that the person who died gave them a gift, how do you prove it — or even disprove it? The executors of the Marlon Brando Estate know how tricky this can be. Brando's former chef and personal assistant sued not one, but twice, claiming he gave her valuable gifts.

Of course, even written gifts can cause messy problems and extensive court battles for estates. Perhaps no case in history illustrates this better than the estate of Alfred Bloomingdale.

the TRUE STORY
of ALFRED S. BLOOMINGDALE!

Being the grandson of the founder of the one of the most successful department stores of all time has its perks. Alfred S. Bloomingdale inherited untold millions (to say the least). With his wealth, he co-founded the Diner's Club credit card company, married a wealthy socialite, Betsy (who was good friends with Nancy Reagan), and became a close friend and advisor of Ronald Reagan. He enjoyed fame, fortune, business and political success.

Apparently that was not enough to satisfy Bloomingdale. He also enjoyed a long relationship with a Hollywood model, Vicki Morgan, who was 18 when they met in 1970. Vicki was already married, had a child out of wedlock, and became married and divorced twice more during their affair that lasted twelve years. Bloomingdale enjoyed her company so much that he paid for her luxury Beverly Hills apartment, along with $18,000 a month to support her. He wrote her letters promising future support as well.

Betsy was none too pleased to hear about the financial promise while Bloomingdale was on his death bed with throat cancer (he passed at the age of 66 in 1982). She immediately put a stop to the financial support, even though Vicki claimed Betsy knew of the affair since at least 1974. In fact, Bloomingdale had arranged for a business deal to benefit his mistress. Betsy stopped that as well. Under Bloomingdale's will and trust — which he signed four weeks before he died — Vicki received nothing.

Vicki didn't take the cutoff lightly. She filed a $10 million lawsuit (in today's value, that's more than $22 million) claiming the letters and oral promises entitled her to the lifetime of support, including monthly payments of $10,000. She went public with details of the affair, giving a 234 page deposition in which she described Bloomingdale's sexual preferences. (Let's just say the letters "S" and "M" were mentioned a few times.)

Betsy's attorneys filed a motion to dismiss Vicki's claim, calling her a well-paid prostitute that wasn't entitled to more of the estate's assets. Vicki's lawsuit amounted to sex for hire, they argued, which was illegal. The judge agreed and dismissed the case. Vicki was shaken and flat broke.

She moved from her luxury apartment in Beverly Hills into a cheap condominium unit with an emotionally unstable roommate. Vicki had met the man, Marvin Pancoast, while they were both patients in a mental health center. They had both gone through treatment for depression.

On July 7, 1983, Pancoast snuck quietly into Vicki's bedroom while she slept and beat her to death with a baseball bat. He then walked to a local police station and calmly told an officer that he killed someone. He spent the rest of his life in jail.

Vicki's son, on behalf of her estate, carried on with the lawsuit. His attorney appealed the dismissal and won, allowing the Vicki Morgan Estate to have a jury trial on its claim. The jury then ruled in favor of Vicki Morgan's estate. The jurors determined, based on a letter signed by Bloomingdale on February 12, 1982, that the Bloomingdale Estate owed $200,000 as part of the lifetime of support promise.

Too bad it came too late for Vicki. If she had been able to reach a court victory sooner, she would not have found herself in the situation that led to her unfortunate murder. For Bloomingdale, he was careful to get his estate affairs in order just weeks before his death, but it seems he didn't get his other "affairs" in order.

Have you made any promises to family or friends that need to be clarified in an estate plan?

Avoid a family fight!

There are too many lawsuits to count involving oral promises of money, payments, gifts, and everything else you can think of. They range from million dollar claims, to disputes over who gets the Christmas ornaments. There was one key that made this case different — the letters. Probate laws, including issues of who gets what property and whether someone is owed money, often turn on what is written. If you or a loved one wants to leave something of value outside a will or trust, at the very least, the wishes should be clear and in writing. Of course, there is no reason not to do it the right way and include the gift of bequest to the will or trust. Vague letters and verbal promises need to be interpreted by a court, which can quickly rack up legal fees for your heirs.

Joint ownership —
the good, the bad
and the ugly

Chapter Sixteen

Quiz time: What's the most common way to pass on your legacy? The will. And what are its shortcomings? There's the need for probate court — which is public, time consuming and expensive — as well as the fact that wills don't help you during your own lifetime. What is the better way?

That's right — trusts. But do most people have trusts? No! In fact, most people don't even have wills!

Instead, people try to find a cheap substitute far too often. Many think they can save the expense of hiring an attorney — and still avoid probate court — by taking a shortcut. They think, "Aha! I have it figured out. If I die with assets in my name alone, then they'll be subject to the probate court. So I'm not going to die with anything in only my name." Sounds like a plan, but not a good one. This is called "joint ownership," and it is tricky.

There are two principal types of "joint ownership." A good to way to understand the two kinds of joint ownership is to imagine a pie. The first and most common

What is Joint Ownership?

"Joint ownership" is what lawyers call it when you add someone else's name to your assets such as your bank accounts and home. When one joint owner dies, the survivor generally becomes the only owner without probate court and without a will or trust. Assets held in joint ownership are called "jointly-held assets" or sometimes even, "joint assets." A bank account titled this way would be referred to as a "joint account."

type is called "joint tenants with rights of survivorship" (the exact language may vary slightly from state to state). Most joint assets are held in this manner. This means that when one person dies, the other person (or people) receive(s) everything. In other words, the surviving owner gets to keep the whole pie. Oh, it's good to be the survivor!

The second, less frequent, type of joint ownership is "tenants in common." (Yes, it sounds a little confusing... the one with "common" in the name is actually less common.) With this type of joint ownership, the surviving owner only receives part of the pie. How much? If there are two owners as tenants in common, when one dies, the survivor keeps half of the pie. What about the other half of the pie? The deceased owner's will or trust dictates who receives this half. Likewise, if there are three owners as tenants in common, each owns one-third of the pie.

"Tenants in Common" vs. "Joint Tenants With Rights of Survivorship"

Remember, "Tenants in Common" is when the person who dies second only gets half the pie and is less frequently used. "Joint Tenants With Rights of Survivorship" means the survivor gets the whole pie when the other joint owner dies. This is what most people have when they use joint ownership.

So why is joint tenants with rights of survivorship more common? For bank accounts, they are automatically set up as joint tenants with rights of survivorship, unless the account owners specify they want it held as tenants in common. This isn't always the case for real estate, but most people still don't usually choose tenants in common. As with many other legal principles, the laws on this do vary from state to state, but this is the general trend. Unless otherwise mentioned, when this book refers to joint assets, we are referring to the "whole pie" type of joint ownership.

How do joint assets like this work? Let's

use an example of a mother who we'll call "Mom." We'll give Mom four different children. But Mom is slowing down and getting older. She needs some help and is thinking about what will happen to her assets when she dies. Do you know anyone like this?

Many people like Mom will add the name of a son (we'll call him Sam) to a bank account so he can help write checks and pay bills. Or perhaps Mom signs a new deed, adding her daughter (let's name her Donna) as a joint owner of Mom's house. Why? Often people like Mom don't want the family to worry about probate court after they die. They assume that their son or daughter will do the "right thing" and share the assets with the rest of their children. (Lawyers call this maneuver a "poor man's will").

Now this isn't limited to bank accounts and houses only. Joint ownership can be used with CDs, investment accounts, real estate, stocks, bonds, cars — almost anything that has paperwork stating who owns it.

When Mom decides to do this, and expects Sam and Donna to share the assets with their siblings when Mom dies, what do you think often happens when Mom is gone? That's right, a fight! Sam and Donna may not carry out Mom's wishes after she dies. They may decide to keep the money from the bank account or the house for themselves. Or, maybe Mom really did want Sam to keep the bank account and for Donna to inherit the house, but the other siblings may not like it. This often leads to court battles that can drag on for years, and cost tens of thousands of dollars or more in legal fees. We'll explore these in more detail in Chapter Eighteen.

But that is just the first of many problems with joint ownership. What happens if, during Mom's lifetime, Sam decides to "borrow" some of the money? He may think, "I'll just pay it back later," or "Mom won't even notice it's gone." As a joint owner, Sam usually has the equal right to withdraw money. Many parents do not consider these issues before adding their children's names to their accounts.

Then there is the problem that arises if Donna becomes disabled and Mom wants to sell her home. Unfortunately, Mom would need Donna's signature to do so. What if Donna is not legally able to sign her name because she was in a car accident and is now incompetent? Or worse, what if Donna refuses to sign off? No parent expects that to happen to them, but believe us... it does! Then Mom would be stuck asking permission from a judge for authority to sign Donna's name to the deed so that Mom can sell her own house. In fact, Mom's children could hold her property hostage.

Also, what if Sam or Donna has too much debt or other financial problems? Their creditors can make a claim on Mom's assets. In the case of bankruptcy, the assets risk being lost, or at the very least tied up for months, if not years. What happens if Sam causes a car accident or his wife files for divorce? What if Donna doesn't pay her taxes? All of these very common situations can turn joint ownership into a nightmare.

the TRUE STORY
of THE GREEDY NIECE!

Ana was crushed when her husband passed away. She had spent most of her 78 years of life relying on Vincent for everything. Her English was not strong and she was financially unsophisticated. Ana and Vincent never had children of their own. They did not have a lot of money... just enough to get by, and a home. One of Ana's nieces, Dawn, came by the house the day after Vincent died and offered to help. Dawn cleaned out and took away Vincent's clothes, personal belongings and paperwork. Ana never saw any of it again. Ana did not fully trust Dawn, but no one else was there to help at the time.

A few weeks later, in early July, Dawn and her husband put a piece of paper in front of Ana and told her to sign it. Ana didn't know what it was and wasn't sure she should sign it. But Dawn and her husband were insistent: "Hurry up and sign it" they kept telling her. Dawn had been helping Ana the last few weeks. Ana was reliant on her and did trust her — at least to a point. So she signed it. She felt she had no choice.

Almost 10 years later, Dawn's husband mysteriously appeared at Ana's home and handed her a one-page document. Neither he nor Dawn had been around for quite some time, so the sudden appearance left Ana very confused. She tried to read the document but didn't understand it.

Ana took the paper to the nice man who helped with her taxes. He read it to her and explained that it was a deed to her home, signed just after her husband died. The deed transferred ownership of Ana's house to Ana and Dawn jointly. Ana was almost out of money — she needed to use the equity in her house to take out a loan to pay her bills. The accountant explained to Ana that it

Joint Ownership — the Good, the Bad and the Ugly   161

would be impossible to do so as long as Dawn was listed as a joint owner of the house, unless Dawn agreed to it.

Ana walked back to her car and started to cry. What was she to do? She talked to another niece, who took her to an attorney. The attorney sent a letter to Dawn asking her to sign a new deed relinquishing her interest in Ana's house, but Dawn refused.

The niece then brought Ana to co-author Andrew. Andrew filed a lawsuit for Ana against Dawn to remove Dawn's name from the title to the house. Dawn hired an attorney and fought the lawsuit. She argued that she did nothing wrong and Ana wanted her to have the house. Dawn said Ana was elderly and simply forgot what happened 10 years before when she signed the deed. Dawn felt entitled to it because she had helped Ana and she did not want Ana to take out a loan on her own house. Why not? That would mean less money for Dawn when Ana died.

Inevitably, the case dragged on for months; eventually Ana agreed to pay Dawn several thousand dollars to end the case. It was that or continue to pay legal fees and wait a year or two for the case to go to trial. Although the thought of giving money to Dawn was distasteful, and Ana had a difficult time coming up with the money, she had no choice. Only a jury could determine who was telling the truth, but Ana couldn't afford to wait through the backlog of cases until she could have her day in court. So she settled and got her house back.

As part of the settlement, Dawn signed off on the house, and her named was removed from the title so Ana could take out the loan she needed. Ana never would have placed Dawn's name on the title to her house if she had known what would happen. Andrew was able to resolve the situation, but not without significant cost to Ana.

Whose name is on the title to your home and bank accounts?

Avoid a family fight!

Lawsuits involving what someone intended or understood when they signed a document — especially one many years in the past — are always difficult. No one should sign what he or she does not understand. Just as important, no one should give anyone they don't fully trust power over any of their assets... houses, bank accounts or anything else. Lawyers cost money, and lawsuits take time. Subjecting your assets to joint ownership with someone who may turn out to be untrustworthy is just not worth it. It's far better to do the proper estate planning and protect yourself and your assets the right way.

The will and trust control everything, right?

Chapter Seventeen

Wills and trusts are a great way for people to express their wishes the right way. But that doesn't mean that they are the only way. While using joint ownership is not ideal, it is common.

In fact, even those who do the proper planning — complete with a will and trust — often have joint names on their assets too. Isn't it better when your assets are titled in the name of your trust? Yes! Why? There is no confusion as to who gets what, among other reasons.

Unfortunately, many people simply aren't educated enough. They believe that if they have a will and trust, those documents control. However, the law does not work that way unless your assets are properly titled in the name of the trust. Remember that lesson about funding from Chapter Seven? Michael Jackson's family does! If your bank account lists the owners as "Mom and Sam," then it is a joint account, which means Sam will usually get the money when Mom dies — not Mom's Trust.

"But wait," you may say, "Mom's Trust says that all bank accounts — even joint ones — are controlled by the Trust. And the Trust says that all of Mom's children share the money, not just Sam."

In other words, Mom's situation (which is not unusual) involves a trust that says one thing, but a joint bank account that, by law, passes to the person whose name is on the account. What does the family do? Which way is right?

In most states, the name on the joint bank account matters, not the trust language. By law, when one joint account holder dies, the survivor owns the money. The money never finds its way into the trust, so the trust does not control. What about a will instead of a trust? The result remains the same.

Joint accounts aren't the only assets that cause confusion and conflict. It is a frequent practice for people to leave a letter, or list, saying how they want certain items of personal property to pass. In fact, many wills and trusts prepared by competent estate planning attorneys actually mention right in the document that such a list may be prepared and should be followed.

How does this work? "Sam gets the dining room table. The silverware goes to Donna. Billy receives the painting," etc. These types of lists are regularly used.

If done the right way, these written lists will control who gets what property. This is true even if the list includes people who are not mentioned as beneficiaries of the will or the trust.

Of course, sometimes people use this approach the wrong way. When that happens, lists saying who gets what property can cause confusion, just like jointly-held assets, when they are inconsistent with the will or trust. These inconsistencies undermine the entire estate plan and often create conflict.

What is the wrong way to use a list? Glad you asked!

the TRUE STORY
of PRINCESS DIANA'S WISHES!

Lady Di was truly the "People's Princess." Her death in a tragic automobile accident on August 31, 1997 shocked people around the world. Everyone wanted her memory to be honored with dignity and grace. Indeed it was, for the most part.

Unfortunately, the estate of Princess Diana was not handled with the same grace, dignity and class that she exuded in life. Years after her passing, when everyone thought the estate had long since settled, Diana's true wishes came to light.

It began with the criminal trial of one of her closest advisors and confidants. Paul Burrell was her butler. One friend described Burrell as the man Diana trusted to be "the custodian of her life's secrets." He was very devoted, even after Diana passed. Accordingly, Burrell discovered something that shocked him.

A few short days after Diana's death, Burrell was surprised to find her sister, Lady Sarah McCorquodale, and mother, Frances Shand Kydd, in Kensington Palace. Diana had named them as executors of her estate through her will dated June 1, 1993. Rather than simply administering the estate, the pair was in the midst of removing her possessions. Burrell even found them shredding countless letters and other documents that belonged to Diana.

What did Burrell do? He panicked! He could not bear the thought of Diana's treasured memories being callously shredded and discarded with the trash. He gathered boxes of Diana's belongings, loaded them into his car, and hid them in his attic.

The executors were upset. They called for an investigation, which led to a police search of Burrell's home on January 18, 2001. When

300 of Diana's belongings were found, the police charged him with theft and the case went to court.

The matter proceeded to trial in October of 2002. The prosecution originally claimed Burrell had stolen Diana's belongings so he could sell them. After nine days of trial, just before Burrell was to take the stand, the case was quickly dismissed when the Queen herself suddenly "recalled" a conversation with Burrell.

Apparently, Queen Elizabeth II remembered that Burrell had previously informed her Majesty that he would remove certain of Diana's belongings for safekeeping. Rumors flew about the Queen wanting to keep dark family secrets from coming to light at the trial.

Reportedly, there were hidden letters, secret tapes, and other evidence of infidelity, scandal and even murder covered up by the royal family. Some in the press speculated that Burrell was going to testify about these secrets, and the Queen had the case dismissed to keep him from revealing them on the witness stand.

With all of these shocking rumors, there was one family secret that seemed tame by comparison. In fact, it almost escaped notice entirely, even though it was disclosed publicly in the Burrell trial.

During the trial, Burrell's lawyers revealed a "letter of wishes" written by Diana and signed on June 1, 1993 — the same day as the will. This letter included the following instruction:

I would like you to divide, at your discretion, my personal chattels between my sons and my godchildren, in the division of three quarters of value to my sons and one quarter to my godchildren.

This revelation was significant. "Chattels" means personal belongings. In other words, it was Diana's wish that one-quarter of her personal property be split among her 17 godchildren. Do you think her sister and mother honored these wishes? Surprisingly, they did not.

Instead, Diana's sister and mother gave the 17 godchildren one trinket each to remember Diana by. Each item had sentimental value only, with no monetary significance, and included commercially available watercolor paintings, an incomplete tea set, and china figurines.

The parents of the godchildren were, by and large, shocked. They were not even aware of the existence of the "letter of wishes." Diana's sister and mother had successfully petitioned the court to have the letter thrown out, on what some reported to be a legal loophole. The letter was found to be invalid, despite a provision in the will itself directing that the separate letter be honored.

Given the vastness of Diana's belongings, the value of these "personal chattels" was considerable. Estimates placed the monetary worth at 100,000 pounds per godchild. Instead of this relative fortune, each child received only a "grubby trinket," according to one of their parents.

Clearly, Diana did not write this letter of wishes without good reason. Yet it was almost completely ignored by her executors and the court. Had Diana been more careful with her estate planning, her wishes could have been honored.

Have you done something to undermine your estate planning documents?

Avoid a family fight!

Make sure your wishes are clear in your will or trust. Otherwise, your instructions may be ignored. Do not rely on other documents to express your intent. The will, or trust, must state how the property is to pass. While referring to a separate list of property is permissible, such a list should be very specific, not general. If you want certain items to pass to select people, a list referenced in the will (or trust) can suffice. But if you want to direct how significant portions of your estate will pass, do not rely on a separate letter or list. Princess Diana's approach led to confusion and placed executors in a difficult position.

It is especially problematic when the letter or list uses words like "desire" or "in their discretion." These make it seem like the wishes are suggestions, not instructions, which executors might be legally permitted to ignore. Make all your instructions clear in the will or trust; do not rely on desire and discretion unless you truly want your executor to decide for you.

the TRUE STORY
of THE HUSBAND WHO DIDN'T MEAN TO DIE FIRST!

It's not unusual for people to write letters or express their wishes in a way that conflicts with their will or trust, like Princess Di. But it's even more common for people to prepare a will or trust, but also keep assets held jointly. Both can cause big problems, as in this case.

Anthony knew his wife Ellen was not well. She suffered from advanced dementia, likely due to Alzheimer's disease. She lived in a nursing home and needed a great deal of help.

Anthony and Ellen accumulated a lot of wealth over their many years together. This included their house, worth nearly half a million dollars, and an investment account held with a large brokerage firm, worth $1.5 million more. Anthony decided to spread their wealth among many nieces, nephews and charities when both he and Ellen died. They had no children of their own. So Anthony visited an attorney and prepared a trust. He signed letters saying he wanted all of their property to be assigned into the trust and pass just as the trust described. But he never mailed these letters.

Instead, he kept everything he owned titled in the name of Anthony and Ellen, jointly as husband and wife, not in the name of his trust. Anthony apparently believed he had time to take care of it later. Ellen's doctors did not expect her to live long. So, rather than funding the trust immediately... which he could have done and still taken care of Ellen through the trust... Anthony waited. And of course, a problem arose.

Anthony needed surgery, and it did not go well. He died unexpectedly. Ellen clearly was not competent to handle the finances and she did not have a trust of her own. So what happened?

It turns out that Ellen did have a will. A very old will — from 1970 — but a will nonetheless. And that will left everything to her favorite nephew, Donald. When Ellen died not long after Anthony, an attorney contacted Donald and told him about the will and the trust. Only this attorney did not tell Donald everything. Donald did not know that the brokerage firm (which held the investments worth $1.5 million) had already allowed the trustee of Anthony's trust to take the accounts out of Ellen's name and move them into the trust. The trustee also sold Anthony and Ellen's house, which Ellen did not need. In other words, Anthony's trustee followed the language of the trust and ignored the fact that the brokerage account and house were jointly titled with Ellen.

Because they were joint assets, both should have remained in Ellen's name after Anthony died, not Anthony's trust. The brokerage company should not have allowed the trustee to do this transfer, but it did. Because Ellen was not competent, and then died shortly thereafter, no one stopped to question what Anthony's trustee was doing.

After the attorney contacted Donald, he thought something was fishy. Donald then hired co-author Andrew to investigate the case. Andrew discovered what had

Appeals

After every trial or hearing which concludes a lawsuit or other legal proceeding, either party has the right to file an "appeal." This means that the case will be reviewed by a higher court. A panel of judges (usually three at the first appellate level) looks over what the first judge decided and may accept or "affirm" the decision, "reverse" it, or send the case back for a new trial. Appeals are always costly and time consuming. They can take 2 or 3 years... and that's the first appeal. There also is a second appellate court, usually called the Supreme Court of the particular state, to which the losing side can file another appeal.

happened and the mistakes that were made. But, by that time, the money from the sale of the house was already gone... distributed to beneficiaries through Anthony's trust. Luckily, the $1.5 million investment account was still in place. But Andrew had to act quickly. He filed three separate lawsuits on Donald's behalf. After years of legal maneuvering and appeals to Michigan's Court of Appeals and then the Supreme Court, Andrew and Donald prevailed. In fact, every judge in each of the courts who reviewed the case ruled in their favor — 11 judges out of 11.

Because the brokerage account was a joint asset between Ellen and Anthony, Ellen became the rightful owner the moment Anthony died. Her will, not Anthony's trust, determined who received the money. Anthony undermined his own trust by waiting to fund the joint assets into it, so his wishes as expressed in the trust had to be ignored.

Have you undermined your trust by waiting to fund it?

Avoid a family fight!

If you have a trust, fund it. Move all of your assets into the trust, unless an attorney tells you not to do so for liability concerns or tax reasons. Joint assets will not pass through your trust when you die, at least in most cases. You must change the title on the assets to the name of the trust.

Anthony could have moved his assets into his trust, if he wanted to, and still protected Ellen. By not doing so, he left it up to Ellen's will to determine how the assets were to be distributed — but only after years of litigation and appeals. If you or your loved ones have a trust, make sure it is funded properly. Leaving assets held jointly instead of in the trust only causes problems.

How Conveeeenient!

Chapter Eighteen

Shortcuts can seem convenient. But sometimes they make things nearly impossible later on. If you're making bread for your family but don't let it rise, they won't end up with as much bread as you'd hoped. The same applies when you cut corners in preparing your estate plan... your loved ones won't end up with as much bread as you may expect.

By now you know that using joint ownership (like adding someone's name to a bank account or a deed to a house) is not a good shortcut to estate planning, even though many people think that it's more convenient. Who doesn't love the idea of something being convenient, right? But when we try a shortcut and it actually works to our detriment, then we probably won't love the idea so much.

Let's return to our example of the fictitious Mom and her children. Remember, she put Sam's name on her bank account and Donna's name on her house.

To Mom, adding her kids' names to these assets may have seemed convenient because it saved her a trip to the attorney's office, but remember, it usually means that Sam can keep the joint bank account and Donna would own the home when Mom dies. That leaves Mom's other children out in the cold.

So what happens after Mom dies if she added Sam and Donna's names only as a convenience, and not because she wanted them to keep the assets for themselves at the time of her death? That's when the law allows the other children to say, "Hey! We want our share of the bread too!" And if those children go to court, they can often convince the judge to rule that Sam and Donna have to share the assets with them. But, like many family feuds that end up in court, these lawsuits can be tricky... especially when real estate is involved.

What are Accounts of Convenience?

This is a legal exception to the general rule of joint ownership passing to the survivor. It applies when an account holder or property owner adds someone's name for the sake of convenience only, not so the person will keep the money or property. Some states use differing terminology for this legal doctrine, especially with respect to real estate, but the principal is the same.

This legal principle is often referred to as "accounts of convenience."

How does an "account of convenience" legal theory work? The person arguing that the joint owner's name was added only for convenience sake, and not so the joint owner could keep the property, has to convince the judge or jury that the decedent didn't intend to give the property solely to the joint owner. If they are successful, then the joint owner has to share the assets. In our example, Sam and Donna's siblings would have to take Sam and Donna to court to make this argument. They would have to go to court even if Mom had a will or trust that split everything equally between all of Mom's children.

Got it? It all comes down to the intent of why the joint owner's name was added to an account or deed. But how do you prove what Mom really intended? Keep in mind that by the time this goes to court, Mom is either mentally incompetent or has passed away.

How about looking at Mom's will or trust? After all, aren't those documents created to show someone's intent? Yes, they are.

In fact, it happens all the time that someone has a will or trust splitting everything equally between their heirs, but has separate joint accounts or property. In this instance, the language of a will or trust can sometimes show the true intent of the joint ownership and support an "account of convenience" legal claim.

But, this approach won't always work. The timing of when Mom signed the will or trust is critical. If she signed the will or trust before she created the jointly owned asset, then the will or trust may be good evidence of her intent. If, however, Mom signed the will or trust after adding a joint owner, then courts usually won't even consider these documents. Why? Because what matters is Mom's state of mind when the joint account was created and not what comes after.

Think about this for a moment. If Mom opens a joint account with Sam, and then a few years later creates a will or trust, then she should withdraw her money from the joint account so that the will or trust can control the money. Mom could have done so (if she was competent, of course). The fact that she didn't suggests that she didn't want her will or trust, created later, to control.

If Mom intended the jointly owned account or property to go to all of her children equally, as she expressed in her will or trust, why did she use joint ownership in the first place? Often, the answer is that Mom did not understand the legal consequences of adding Sam and Donna's names to her assets. Too bad our fictitious Mom didn't have this book to read!

The big question remains: what did Mom really intend? The honest answer: no one really knows. It's a huge problem for families faced with contradictory documents — a will or trust on one hand, and a joint bank account, car title or deed, or even a "letter of wishes" (as in the Princess Di story) on the other hand.

It's tricky stuff, we know. It's never easy to figure out what a dead person really intended. In fact, sometimes it's tough even when the person is still alive, such as an elderly person with memory problems... especially if he or she has dementia or Alzheimer's disease.

So don't take that shortcut! Let your bread rise fully... and make sure your parents and other loved ones know this too. Put everything in your trust, or if you don't have a trust, leave everything in your name alone (or with your spouse only). Don't create joint accounts or other contradictory documents that show a different intent. Why do that to your family? You created that trust or will for a reason.

the TRUE STORY
of the GIRLFRIEND WHO SHOT HER BOYFRIEND!

One of the more interesting disputes over joint accounts arose in connection with a murder case in Florida. Michelle Julia shot and killed her long time boyfriend, John "Jack" Russo, on May 19, 2006. She claimed self-defense and that he had been abusing her for years. In fact, Julia said Russo was chasing her with a long knife when she shot him.

Russo's family didn't believe a word of it. They claimed she staged it all for the money. Jack Russo was worth around $20 million. Apparently, he had added Julia's name to an investment account just weeks before the shooting. How much? A cool half million dollars.

The family said Russo was about to leave her and was dating someone else in secret. So of course, the family filed a claim under Florida's Slayer Statute (remember the Slayer Statute from Chapter Eight?). As you may recall, the law penalizes murderers so they can't inherit money from someone they intentionally kill. In this case, the criminal investigation into the shooting was inconclusive and never resolved; Julia was not charged with a crime.

Accordingly, it was up to the family to prove that she shot him intentionally and not because of self-defense. The brokerage account presented an added quirk however. Even if the family's Slayer Statute claim succeeded, Julia would still get half of the brokerage account. Under the law in Florida, a "slayer" receives "tenants in common" rights under a joint account. The law does not allow a killer to receive the full "joint tenants with rights of survivorship" rights, which means that he or she can't receive the full amount of the account. (If you've forgotten what these terms mean... tenants in common means that the joint owner receives half of the jointly-owned asset, and not the entire asset. You can turn back to Chapter 16 to review the different types of ownership.)

In other words, even if she did kill him on purpose, and not because of self-defense, she still would get half. Unbelievable, huh! Because of this, Julia's attorneys filed a motion asking the court to let her withdraw one-half of the money from the account. The attorney representing the estate (and therefore representing the family's interests) opposed the motion. How did they oppose it? By arguing that Jack Russo did not intend for Julia to receive everything. Russo only added her name to the joint account because he trusted her. Russo and Julia had always kept their money separate and this account contained Russo's money.

The family felt Julia's name was added as a convenience only; for example, she accessed the account only when Russo permitted her to. The probate judge agreed with the Russo family and did not allow Julia to have the money.

But she wasn't about to walk away from at least $250,000 so easily! She appealed to the Court of Appeals. The judges who reviewed the case agreed that Russo did not intend to give the money to Julia because there was no evidence he intended to make a gift to her. However, both the probate judge and the Court of Appeals applied the wrong legal test. Julia asked the three appellate judges to reconsider their ruling, and they did. They looked at the case a second time and ruled that Russo's family had the legal burden to provide evidence and prove there was no gift. This is what the law provides — because this was a joint account, Julia as the survivor gets the money unless the family challenging it proves it was an account of convenience only. Without evidence that Russo added Julia's name for this purpose, and not because he wanted her to receive the money, she would be entitled to at least half of it — even if she did murder him.

The problem was that Russo was dead, so coming up with that evidence was very difficult. As of the date this edition went to print, the case hadn't been resolved yet. Currently it seems tipped in Julia's favor. Check TrialAndHeirs.com for the latest information on this and other on-going stories.

Have you, or someone you love, considered adding another person's name to a bank account to help with bill paying?

Avoid a family fight!

Lawsuits based on accounts of convenience are usually difficult to prove. This can be true even in cases where an older person adds the name of someone younger who they trust to help pay bills and manage money. Without good evidence in favor of a "convenience account," then the person whose name is on the joint account will be allowed to keep it. People often document their true intent through a will or trust, but may not help if they were created after the time the name was added. Remember, the law looks at the moment the property was made joint, not what the person intended months or even years later. There are far better ways for one person to allow another to help them with finances instead of resorting to jointly held property. Trusts, powers of attorney, and even guardianships or conservatorships will accomplish the same goal without creating confusion about whether the name was added for convenience or not.

One other point to remember... when exploring whether to challenge a joint account or other jointly-held property, don't forget about mental incompetence and undue influence claims (we covered those in Section III). Those very same legal claims can also be used to help heirs who want joint property shared with everyone, not just the person lucky enough to be named as a joint owner. But only in the right circumstances. As we explored in those chapters, telling the court you think the deceased loved one was incompetent or someone influenced them can be emotionally difficult, and will require proof that may be hard to find. But you don't want to forget those options when fighting over joint assets.

Hurray! My name is on the life insurance

Chapter Nineteen

It's a sad time for any family when a loved one dies. Of course, in many families, there are those who secretly celebrate the loss. More people than you may expect!

The first question these people often ask after "Can I see the will?" is "What about the life insurance?" Well, what about it? How does it work when someone dies?

Life insurance is a prominent example of an asset that uses a "beneficiary designation" instead of titles that determine ownership, like bank accounts, real estate or cars. Other examples are annuities, Individual Retirement Accounts (IRAs), and certain other investments.

Whenever a financial product of this nature includes a beneficiary, then whoever is listed as the beneficiary gets the money. The same rule would apply to a bank account that is held "payable on death." This, too, works just like an insurance policy.

When you purchase an insurance policy or one of these investments, you (or the agent or financial planner who sold it to you) fill out a form that includes a spot for

What is Beneficiary Designation?

A "beneficiary designation" is a way to pass certain assets onto heirs without a will, trust or probate court. This only applies for assets that have forms that allow you to name a beneficiary, usually when the policy or investment is purchased. You can usually change your beneficiary designation, as long as you are competent to do so.

who will be the beneficiary of that policy or investment when you pass away. Because it's so easy to fill it out, do you think it's no big deal? Wrong! Be careful whose name you write down when you fill out this form.

Think back to the time you were a kid. Did you ever go through a phase where you wanted to make absolutely sure that none of your siblings or friends took your stuff? Did you write your name on your toys so everyone knew they belonged to you? If you did, at least in your mind, that meant the toy was yours, and only yours, no matter what! (If only grown-up laws were so straightforward). Beneficiary designations work like this. If your name is on it, you get to keep it. But wait, there is an "unless" coming up in a moment.

Assets that use beneficiary designations are similar to joint assets. The will or trust does not control these assets, unless you fill out the beneficiary forms the right way. So what is the right way? If you have a life insurance policy and want your trust to control who gets it, you must name your trust as the beneficiary of the insurance policy. If you want the will to control, then you name your estate as the beneficiary. If you're not sure how to accomplish this, ask an estate planning attorney to be safe. Annuties, IRAs and other investments with a beneficiary designation all work like this. How you fill in the form when it asks for your beneficiary is crucial. So think about it before you write down a name!

When this form is not completed as it should be — and Mom names Sam as the beneficiary under an insurance policy — the insurance proceeds will go to Sam, not the beneficiaries named under Mom's trust or will. In fact, even if Sam is the successor trustee of the trust, or the executor of the estate, he still receives the money (as long as Sam's name, by itself, is listed as the beneficiary of an insurance policy). If Mom wants Sam to receive it on behalf of the trust, she must mention the trust in the insurance documents that she fills out when naming a beneficiary. How would she do so? Usually, she should write, "Sam, as Successor Trustee of the Mom Trust."

But, once again, not everything is black and white. There are exceptions to the general rule. (Here comes that "unless!") The very same exceptions we discussed with joint assets in the last Chapter can apply to insurance policies and other assets that have beneficiary designations. When someone purchases the policy or investment and intends the person named as beneficiary to share it with others, the recipient can be forced to split up the money, but only following a successful "account of convenience-type" lawsuit in court. Once again, these cases aren't easy to win because you have to prove what someone intended, and that person isn't around to tell everyone what was in his or her mind.

Also, as with joint assets, the incompetence and undue influence challenges can work with assets that have beneficiary designations. If it is proven that Mom wasn't competent — or was tricked or coerced when she filled out the insurance beneficiary form — then the law essentially says to ignore the beneficiary designation. Instead, the money will pass to the decedent's estate, usually.

But these are not the only exceptions. Other legal theories can apply to overcome the beneficiary designation in unusual circumstances. This is one of the many areas where an attorney's advice can be crucial.

the TRUE STORY
of WHITNEY HOUSTON!

Whitney Houston is no stranger to family fights in court. In 2002, the entertainment company owned by her father, John Houston, sued her. John Houston said publicly that his company was owed $100 million and he expected his daughter to repay it. He died in February of 2003, and the case was dismissed not long thereafter. Reportedly, Whitney Houston did not attend her father's funeral service or burial.

John's wife, Barbara, filed her own lawsuit against Whitney in December of 2008. Whitney was the sole beneficiary of a $1 million life insurance policy of her late father.

Barbara Houston claims that Whitney had agreed with her father that the money would be used to pay off a mortgage that Whitney held over John and Barbara Houston's home. Apparently, Whitney lent her father $723,000 in 1990 and this loan was secured by a mortgage against his house, payable to Whitney. Barbara's lawsuit alleges that the life insurance was purchased to pay off this mortgage, and the remaining balance was to be turned over to Barbara.

Apparently, even though five years had passed since John Houston died, Whitney never gave any money to Barbara. Barbara also says in her lawsuit that Whitney did not even release the mortgage. So did Whitney give in? We all know she has plenty of money already, right?

Heck No! Instead, Whitney filed a counterclaim. She claimed the life insurance was intended to repay Whitney for other money she had lent her father, not payoff the mortgage. To top it off, Whitney also counter-sued her late father's wife to force her to repay the mortgage. And she even wanted interest on the mortgage... $1.6 million in total.

But there was an encore to the fireworks! Whitney decided to use the countersuit as a prime opportunity to slam her "step-mother." She pointed out that Barbara was 40 years younger than her father, how she dated her father for three years before the divorce from Whitney's mother, and how Barbara met John as a maid cleaning his house. Remember, lawsuits are public record, so Whitney knew that airing all of this dirty laundry would be in public.

So who is telling the truth? Did John Houston really want Whitney to keep the money as a repayment for other money owed, or had he trusted Whitney to pay off the mortgage and give the rest of the money to Barbara?

The problem is, we don't know. John shouldn't have relied on naming Whitney as his life insurance beneficiary without an agreement or other writing clarifying why he did so. Or, even better, he should have created a trust, named it as a beneficiary of the insurance, and then his trust could have directed exactly who should receive the money and why.

Instead of clearly documenting his intent, John took a shortcut. Now, because of his shortcut, his wife and famous daughter are bearing their nails and teeth at one another, in public.

Once again, this is an ongoing case. Be sure to visit TrialAndHeirs. com to keep up with Whitney and Barbara's next moves.

Who is named as the beneficiary of your life insurance, IRA or annuity?

Avoid a family fight!

Never, ever name someone as a beneficiary of your life insurance policy unless you want that person to keep the money. It's not worth leaving it up to faith and trust. If the life insurance has significant value (which most life insurance policies do), create a trust, and name the trust as your beneficiary on the insurance policy. Then you can dictate exactly how the money is to be split, and under what conditions.

Once you die, the beneficiary of your insurance can claim the money immediately, without notifying anyone else and without going through probate court. If the rest of your family has to start a lawsuit to get the money back, they have to sue right away or the beneficiary can collect (and spend) the money before anyone else even knows it's gone. In Whitney's case, she has the assets to repay the $1 million if a court orders her to do so. But in most families, this is not the case. Whenever families fight over who really should have the insurance proceeds, they have no choice but to file lawsuits quickly before the money is gone.

It was a gift — really!

Chapter Twenty

Asset disputes come in many shapes and sizes. Often the most contentious start with the most simple of legal concepts — a gift.

At least, one would think the legal concept is simple. What can be complicated about a gift? It's really basic, right? Grandma gives you a present, beautifully wrapped with colorful paper, ribbons and a giant bow. You eagerly tear into it to discover... socks and underwear! Just what you wanted.

Was this a legal gift? Yes. But why? Because Grandma's present met all three of the legal elements required for a valid gift. First, she had the intent to give you the socks and underwear. Second, she delivered them to you. Finally, you accepted the gift — and, yes, it still counts as an acceptance if you only did so because your mother would ground you if you didn't.

Still waiting for the complicated part? Here it comes. How do you really know "intent?" How do you deliver something that can't be handed over like socks and underwear? What does it mean to deliver real estate or a bank account? And does anyone ever fail to "accept" a gift?

Things become especially murky when no one else saw the supposed gift. When

A gift is a gift right?

Sounds easy enough, why would anyone be confused about what a gift is? You can always count on lawyers to make basic concepts sound complicated. For something to qualify as a gift under the law, you need three things: Intent, delivery and acceptance.

Mom is gone, and Sam says that Mom gave him her wedding ring because she wanted Sam's wife to have it, what does the rest of the family do when they all think Sam is lying? They sue, that's what they do. Sometimes the biggest fights are over the smallest items, and disputed gifts often take center stage. Wills and trusts seldom mention individual items of personal property, such as a coin collection, treasured photo album or wedding ring. There are no titles to determine who should get them.

There is an old adage among attorneys that possession is nine-tenths of the law. Often families can sit down and sort through these problems without a big fight. But in those danger zones of sibling rivalries and second marriages, divvying up the pots, pictures and paintings is not as easy as you may think. "Dad wanted me to have the painting of the dogs playing poker." "Mom handed me her necklace and said she wanted me to keep it... really!"

The question of "intent" in a disputed gift case is never easy to solve. "Delivery" is usually easier, except when the actual asset in question can't be delivered. In those cases, a token is usually required (such as a deed for a house, or keys to a car). "Acceptance" is usually straightforward because the law presumes someone claiming they were given something actually did accept it. However, all three elements must occur during the giver's lifetime.

That is, unless the gift was intended to take effect only on death. When that happens, it makes the situation even more complicated. When any single element is questioned — intent, delivery or acceptance — families often end up fighting in court.

the TRUE STORY
of MARLON BRANDO!

Respected by many as the leading actor of his generation, 80-year-old Marlon Brando died on July 1, 2004, with a host of ailments including dementia and lung failure. A mere 13 days before that, Brando changed his will by signing a codicil that appointed new executors. By that time, Brando's physical condition had deteriorated to the point that he did not even leave his bedroom, much less his home.

The codicil replaced Brando's assistant of 50 years as well as his business manager of 40 years with new people to administer his estate. Brando's $21 million estate quickly became embroiled in many different legal proceedings, including a sexual harassment and wrongful termination lawsuit, several creditor claims, website disputes and a fight about whether a Brando chair could be sold without permission. But perhaps the most unusual of the legal disputes involved Brando's former caregiver and personal assistant.

Angela Borlaza began working for Brando in 1995 as a cook. Eventually, she ran his household and considered herself to be Brando's "major domo." She was not pleased when Brando signed the codicil to his will because she was not allowed in the room when it happened.

Some who were close to Brando claimed that Borlaza had exercised too much control over Brando and he felt trapped. On the other hand, they also said Brando also wanted his bedroom padlocked at his death so no one would steal the buttons off his shirt. Whether Brando's fears were real or imagined, one thing was clear — Borlaza had no control over the estate.

But that doesn't mean she left quietly. Soon after Brando died, the new estate executors fired Borlaza and instructed her to vacate her home located in the San Fernando Valley, in California, which was owned by Brando. The estate sold the house for $627,000. Borlaza was not happy.

She sued the estate for $2 million, saying that Brando had given the house to her. Borlaza said Brando has only kept it in his name for tax reasons. The executors fought the claim. They argued Brando never intended to make a gift, among other defenses. The two sides went before a mediator and tried to settle the claim. According to court records, the settlement efforts worked. Borlaza settled her claim for $125,000 in December of 2006.

She was not finished, however. Borlaza sued the Brando Estate again in August of 2007, this time alleging that Brando had promised her that his estate and a company he owned would continue to employ her for many years after his death. In other words, she again claimed Brando intended to give her something of value — the promise of continued employment.

But, to spice up the second lawsuit, Borlaza argued that the new executors did not have legal authority to break this promise because the deathbed codicil was, in fact, a forgery. Borlaza even had an ally this time. When Brando's son, Christian, died in January of 2008, Christian's ex-wife also sued the estate raising the same claim of forgery. Borlaza's second lawsuit, like the first one, settled, but the amount has not been made public.

It is very likely that she accepted an amount much less than what she sued for, as was the case with the first lawsuit. Whether Brando ever really promised her the house and long-term employment is very much in doubt, but that is the nature of "gift" claims. When the only person who can really refute it is dead, legal challenges based on gifts or other oral promises cause headaches for everyone. It is very hard to prove with any certainty what he or she truly intended. Did Brando really make these gifts to Borlaza, or did she make it all up? She is the only one alive who can really answer that question.

Are you worried about your family fighting over a questionable gift?

Avoid a family fight!

Anyone worried about fights over personal property items should leave a list or other writing indicating who gets what. If you are the recipient of a gift and want to avoid conflict, ask Mom or Dad to write down their wishes, and sign and date the document to verify the intent to make a gift. With more substantial assets like real estate, there is never a reason to rely on a gift. Those assets should be passed through a will or trust. Of course, if there is a valid gift of real estate, it should be done with a proper deed, not a verbal promise.

On the other hand, if you are the one in charge of an estate or trust and are worried about greedy family members, friends or caregivers coming out of the woodwork claiming there was a gift when you believe there really wasn't one, what can you do? Nothing is easy, that's for certain. You should fight the challenge if it makes financial sense and settle if it doesn't. While legal claims based on gifts seldom prevail in full, they do cause both sides to incur legal fees and often lead to settlements. This doesn't mean to cave anytime someone extends his or her hand and asks for a gift. Rather, a prudent business decision should be made about whether it will be costlier to fight or settle. Of course, you should talk to an experienced attorney before making any decision of this nature.

Ideas to Spark Family Dialogue

Family disputes often start over assets, including personal property, bank accounts and real estate. This is especially true when there are confusing or misleading documents. As always, the best prescription is clear and consistent instructions properly documented through a trust — or at least a will — as part of a complete estate plan. But the trust must be funded with the assets, instead of joint ownership, for the trust to properly work.

If your parents or other loved ones have a trust, ask them how their assets are held or titled. The trust, through its trustee(s), should be listed as the owner of bank accounts, real estate, investments, and anything else with a title (even cars and boats). That is, unless your lawyer or accountant tells you not to for tax or liability reasons. And it is not enough for assets to start out in the name of the trust but be changed later. Make sure your parents understand the titles must stay that way.

If your parents don't have a trust, and won't get one for any reason, then their accounts should be left in their individual names. Adding a name of one or more children invites problems, including family conflict.

"But I trust Sam," Mom may say. "He helps me write my checks." This same convenience can be accomplished without the complications inherit in joint ownership. With a proper power of attorney Mom can appoint Sam to help pay the bills without changing the title to her bank accounts.

Worried that someone may convince your elderly parent to put his name on an account? Talk to your loved ones about the danger, and check the titles on their bank statements and other assets regularly. That way you can spot a change. It also helps if Mom writes down her intent before adding Sam's name to the account. If it is clear ahead of time that any changes are for convenience only, not so Sam can keep the account, then it will help resolve the matter if conflict erupts down the road.

And don't forget about the life insurance. You think Whitney Houston and her step-mother enjoyed fighting publicly in court? Remind your loved ones to be careful when naming a beneficiary to life insurance, annuities and IRAs.

Encouraging your loved one to write down his or her intent also helps for gifts and other personal property wishes. But it should be done the right way — as part of a comprehensive estate plan. Don't end up like those involved in the Marlon Brando Estate. Talk to your parents about why verbal gifts or telling someone what they want is not enough. Of course, most parents feel they can trust their children, but the temptation to stray is too great when the parent is gone. Verbal gifts and oral wishes rarely are legally valid, but they can still lead to a big fight.

SECTION V

THE EXECUTOR IS SCREWING IT UP!

With every will and trust, there's a way...

for a fight to start even when the person who died did everything right. Many court disputes have nothing to do with what someone wanted or intended.

Instead, these battles arise when the person in charge of the estate or trust doesn't do what he or she is supposed to do (or at least, that's what someone thinks).

Chapter Twenty-One discusses how, for executors and trustee, IT'S A JOB, NOT A WALK IN THE PARK. They have legal duties they must uphold, and they are required to protect the beneficiaries. It's not always easy. Just ask Jerry Garcia's widow, who administered his estate for 8 years, fending off too many people to count who claimed they were owed money.

When the job isn't done right, courts have to start MANAGING MISMANAGEMENT, explored in Chapter Twenty-Two. Those in charge of Rosa Parks' legacy know this all too well. Her estate was tied up in court over questions of mismanagement for years.

HOW ABOUT SOME LOYALTY? Chapter Twenty-Three discussed the obligation that executors must follow to put the interests of the beneficiaries above their own. It's far from easy at times, as Doris Duke's alcoholic former butler and estate executor could tell you, since he was removed after a lengthy court fight.

Sometimes executors and trustees go even further. Many heirs want to shout "HEY - HE'S STEALING!" You'll learn, in Chapter Twenty-Four, some of the subtle and not so subtle ways that stealing can occur, and how to watch your back.

But of course, the best way to prevent this is to make sure that you CHOOSE WISELY. Chapter Twenty-Five will tell you how to decide who should be executor or trustee if there's potential friction in your family, such as in second-marriage situations like Ted Kennedy's family.

Finally, after reading Chapter Twenty-Six, you'll stop losing sleep thinking "I DON'T WANT TO BE SUED." Open communication and working with a good attorney are just the start. Too bad Martin Luther King, Jr.'s son didn't follow this advice; he could have avoided a messy family court fight.

As ugly as the MLK JR. Estate became, it pales in comparison to the mess caused by the lead singer of INXS when he placed too much trust in his administrators.

the TRUE STORY
of INXS LEAD SINGER MICHAEL HUTCHENCE!

INXS was one of the most successful Australian rock bands of all time, maintaining worldwide popularity in the 1980s and early 90s. Lead singer Micheal Hutchence drove the band's success, until he was found dead in a Sydney, Australia hotel room at the age of 37. His death on November 22, 1997 was officially ruled a suicide by hanging, although some suspected foul play. His body was nude, there was no suicide note, and certain other evidence suggested unlawful intent.

Hutchence's will seemed fairly straightforward. He wanted one-quarter of a million dollars (U.S. value) to pass to Amnesty International and Greenpeace, each. His only child was to receive one-half of the remainder, with the rest divided between his girlfriend, mother, father, brother and sister. There was one rather substantial problem. Despite estimates of ten to twenty million dollars — if not more — Hutchence's estate held virtually nothing. And it took eight years for the administrators to reach this conclusion.

No shortage of oddities surrounded the estate. On February 13, 1999, a London newspaper, the Courier-Mail, ran a story following a lengthy investigation. It reported that Hutchence had seemingly legitimate business dealings with a company connected to the Italian mafia. Specifically, Harbrick Pty Ltd., directed by a purported mafia family, sold a Gold Coast bowling alley for $2.25 million. This was no ordinary bowling alley... Italy's Gold Coast is one of the wealthiest areas in the world. Hutchence had personally inspected this bowling alley and told tenants there that he was buying it. (There's no word on what he bowled during his inspection though).

Yet the bowling alley property was never put in Hutchence's name. Rather, it and many other properties were placed into a series of eight companies and related trusts. Most of these were "offshore" trusts and companies, in the Caribbean for example. The companies and trusts were so complicated and extensive that there was no solid proof that any of the properties ever belonged to Hutchence. Yet he told family members he had purchased them. Is it possible that Hutchence was playing a "shell game," or was he the being played by his financial advisors?

The family sued the administrators of these various companies and trusts in 1997, claiming they breached their duties and mismanaged the assets by failing to turn them over to the estate so they could pass pursuant to Hutchence's will. They racked up $500,000 in legal fees and court costs. The case was so complicated that they felt no choice but to settle, in 1999, for an amount that wasn't even enough for them to recover their legal fees.

Hutchence's sister, Tina Hutchence, and mother, Patricia Glassop, wrote a book called Just A Man (published in 2000) that described how the process was very expensive, because of the multiple claims against 14 different defendants. They wrote that the Australian legal system required the family to have three attorneys at every court hearing. In the end, while the case settled for a confidential amount, they wrote that the lawsuit was "incredibly frustrating." Glassop later said publicly that the family received "absolutely nothing" from Hutchence's assets, except a few small items. She personally received "a couple of small bowls, some awards and a big poster."

Despite this settlement, the estate still didn't end for quite some time. It was not until August 2, 2005, that the estate administrators filed a detailed report concluding that the estate was broke, in large part, due to $670,000 in legal fees. One of the administrators reported in 1999 that the estate had $1.2 million at the time, which was a fraction of the total assets the family believed Hutchence actually owned. These included three Gold Coast properties worth more than $10 million, a villa in France, a house in London and many more assets — not to mention the extensive INXS royalties.

There were many questions. Like why did Hutchence tell family members he paid one million dollars for one of the properties, only to have an administrator say he was not involved in the purchase, directly or indirectly? And why did the executors sell his custom-made Harley-Davidson motorcycle for $2,000 when it was re-sold a few years later for $61,600? And why would his chosen executors include a self-described international lawyer who isn't licensed to practice law and a bankrupt adviser who failed to pay taxes for 20 years?

And, it gets worse. The executors included three men who were implicated by police in a tax scheme that cost a government agency and bank a total of $22 million. But the case against them was so complicated that prosecutors felt they couldn't handle it. Wow!

There are no good answers, although the administrators did try to offer one explanation. Hutchence's finances were set up exactly as he wished, they said, which was to prevent his "thieving relatives" and "girlfriends" from getting his fortune. If so, it seems he got his wish!

Have you thought long and hard about the best person or people to administer your estate or trust?

Avoid a family fight!

The choice of executor, administrator or trustee is crucial in any estate plan. From the complex, to the very simple, those left in control after death have a great deal of authority and opportunity to engage in wrongdoing. It is important for everyone with any level of assets to name a person through a will or trust; otherwise the court will decide whom to appoint. Don't let that happen to you. You need to choose a person who is best equipped to handle the role and be worthy of your trust.

Did Hutchence choose people he trusted, who truly followed his wishes? Or were there underhanded dealings that forced him to make those choices? Or, maybe, he was tricked into choosing those he thought would do the right thing. We'll likely never know which it was. But we do know his family was left out in the cold. Surely that would not have happened if he chose someone who wanted to protect his child and the others he named as beneficiaries in his will.

It's a job, not a walk in the park

Chapter Twenty-One

When the funeral is over, the friends and out-of-town family members return home and the children and grandchildren are left behind with their sorrow. The last thing anyone wants to worry about is managing the estate or trust. But it's inevitable. It has to be done. It's time to move on with your lives.

And the person named as trustee or estate administrator has the heavy burden of managing the affairs of the loved one who passed, making sure his or her wishes are followed. You owe it to the person who passed to ensure that his or her legacy, built from a lifetime of hard work and savings, goes where it is supposed to go.

When the executor assumes that role, he or she accepts the power and authority that goes with it. At that moment, one important constant always holds true, the person with the power to act also has a legal responsibility. Most states use the term "fiduciary obligation."

It's sort of like the trust placed in a good teacher. Parents of every student count on the teacher to protect, nurture and educate the entire class, not to help some

What is a Fiduciary Obligation?

What does this mouthful mean? Don't be discouraged, it's not that hard. The executor or trustee has a "fiduciary obligation" to act in the best interests of the beneficiaries. A "fiduciary" is one in whom trust and confidence has been placed... both by the person who died and under the law. A fiduciary is legally required to live up to that high level of trust.

and neglect others. Teachers have a great deal of responsibility placed in them and the parents expect teachers to communicate well. Obviously, selling assets and distributing money is a lot different than educating children, but the concept of trust and responsibility applies the same way. That's what a fiduciary obligation is all about.

And this obligation applies both to trustees and to executors. They must be fair and honorable towards all beneficiaries. The law requires them to put the collective best interests ahead of their own. Sounds like basic common sense, right? Of course a trustee or executor is trusted to do what is right for everyone involved in the trust or estate. It should be pretty cut and dry.

By now, you probably realize that there isn't much in this area of law that is easy. Not all is black and white. Questions of grey predominate time and time again. The bottom line is, if you ever become an executor or trustee and have to deal with complications, disagreements, confusion, or substantial assets to manage, you shouldn't go it alone. Similarly, if you are the beneficiary, and you suspect someone has violated the fiduciary duty, the same rule holds true. In both cases, it's time to talk to an experienced probate attorney.

But when should you be worried? Whether you're looking at this from the shoes of a beneficiary or if you're the person in charge wanting to avoid accusations, you need to know the basic legal concepts that apply. There are three basic areas... mismanagement, the duty of loyalty and outright stealing. These three areas are consistent for both trustees and estate administrators. And yes, that holds true even though estates are overseen by probate judges, and trusts usually are not.

Other than court involvement, the basic overall duties are the same. In fact, when there is a dispute surrounding a trust, anyone interested in the trust — trustees and beneficiaries alike (and sometimes, even creditors) — can file a petition or other legal document with the court asking the judge to "take jurisdiction" or supervise the trust.

Court proceedings are common in any estate or trust with complications. In large estates and trusts that have unusual aspects, or when an administrator has difficult heirs to deal with or a confusing estate plan, you can usually count on at least a few disputed questions arising for a probate judge to answer. But even in small or seemingly straightforward estates, judicial help can become necessary. The job of a fiduciary is rarely easy.

In fact, contrary to what many well meaning parents intend by naming their "favorite" child as their executor, they don't realize that it is a burden and not a gift. Many people come to "rue the day" their loved one gave them this gift.

Taking jurisdiction over and supervising estates and trusts

While these words can mean different things in other legal settings, in the world of probate, estates and trusts, these mean that the judge will oversee the estate or trust administration and resolve any conflicts or questions. It allows the judge to help make sure the administrator or trustee does his or her job correctly. The precise level of involvement that a judge takes will vary from state to state, and sometimes from courtroom to courtroom. It's up to the discretion of the judge. In fact, judges can choose whether or not to get involved at all, but someone first has to ask them to.

the TRUE STORY
of JERRY GARCIA!

No one ever said that administering a trust or estate is a walk in the park. Just ask Deborah Koons Garcia. She was the third (and final) wife of Grateful Dead guitarist and front man, Jerry Garcia. He died on August 9, 1995 from heart failure at a drug rehab facility, at age 53. He left behind a vast musical legacy and an estate valued at $15.4 million in 1998. Koons Garcia filed to open the probate in September 1995. Creditors began knocking on her door almost immediately.

In the first three months alone, Koons Garcia was faced with $7.3 million in creditor claims. Some reports peg the total claims at more than $50 million. The problem was that most of the Garcia Estate's value was in royalties and other non-liquid assets. In other words, Koons Garcia had very little cash at her disposal. In fact, Koons Garcia said publicly that her late husband only had a few hundred thousand dollars in the bank. That's not much help when Garcia's second wife asked for $5 million all by herself.

Of course Garcia's widow wasn't about to write a check this big to his ex-wife #2. So the case went to court. Ex-wife #2 Carolyn Adams Garcia (also known as "Mountain Girl") demanded a lifetime of payments from the estate based on a "divorce settlement" that promised her $250,000 a year. With that much money involved, wouldn't you think that Jerry Garcia signed it with the help of a team of lawyers? Even a lifelong hippie would know to do that, right? Not exactly.

A year and a half before he died, Ms. Mountain Girl approached Garcia while backstage at a concert. She presented him with a hand-written document that was only one paragraph long. It said that Garcia was required to pay her this money for the rest of her life.

For all his faults, Garcia was an honorable man. He tried to live up to the agreement and made payments of $400,000 to Mountain Girl while he was alive. His widow obviously wasn't happy with it though. She fought against having to pay it. Why? She said Garcia's judgment was impaired from drugs when he signed it, so it shouldn't count. She even argued the marriage was never legitimate to start with.

Too bad for Koons Garcia, but the judge disagreed. The divorce agreement was held to be valid and the estate was ordered to pay Mountain Girl $5 million.

Koons Garcia didn't give up. She filed an appeal to challenge the judge's ruling. More than three years after Garcia's death, she and Mountain Girl settled for around $1.25 to $1.5 million. A lot of money, sure, but it's certainly better than paying $5 million.

But that didn't end the fun for Koons Garcia. It took another three years, until October, 2001, for the probate court to finally close the estate. By then, thirteen different law firms had been involved, sorting through scores of different claims, including one for $1.3 billion from a woman claiming (falsely, it turned out) that she carried Garcia's secret love child.

Still the battles didn't end. By 2006, Jerry Garcia's youngest daughter, Keelin Noel Garcia (who was the daughter of Garcia's girlfriend in the late 80s and early 90s) started yet another legal proceeding seeking some of Garcia's money.

She sued Koons Garcia and several of the attorneys who administered the estate, claiming she did not receive enough child support. Garcia's will stated that child support obligations to Keelin should be paid before any estate distributions. Keelin felt Koons Garcia and the attorneys violated their fiduciary obligation (there are those words again) to make those payments.

The legal maneuvering appeared to have finally ended in January 2008, when Keelin's lawsuit against Koons Garcia and the attorneys was closed. The details of the resolution were not made public, but records from the United States Patent and Trademark Office show that certain trademarks (including the "Cherry Garcia" trademark to ice cream makers Ben & Jerry) were split 1/3 to Koons Garcia (her share under the will) plus 13.33 percent for Keelin's benefit, with the rest going to a business set up for the heirs. Some have speculated that Keelin received an increased share of the proceeds from these trademarks as a settlement of her lawsuit. (That does make sense... Cherry Garcia is darn good ice cream.)

Clearly, serving as executor for this estate was quite an eye-opener for Koons Garcia. She explained how frustrating it was during a 2008 video interview with the Baltimore Celebrity Examiner (searchable on YouTube.com if you're interested). She described how she went from not knowing what an "executor" was to spending eight years of her life sorting out Jerry Garcia's affairs and protecting his legacy after he died.

Koons Garcia complained about the "huge, huge numbers of hanger-on-ers" who said they were entitled to money because of promises by Garcia during his life. In fact, mostly because of all the time she had to spend dealing with these claimants, Koons Garcia earned a substantial executor fee. She received a salary of $450,000 through 2001 alone, in addition to what she received as a beneficiary of the will.

So the wife of the ultimate hippie became a "professional" executor. That's quite a career change!

Have you done the proper estate planning so the person you chose to administer your estate or trust after you die won't have unnecessary complications?

Avoid a family fight!

The better estate planning someone does in life often correlates to the length and difficulty of administration required after death. If Garcia's affairs weren't left in such a mess, his widow would not have had such a challenging time managing his estate. Protecting your family and legacy after you're gone doesn't end with doing a will or trust. You must continue to work with a good attorney as your life changes and your wishes change with them.

If Garcia had done a proper trust and explicitly stated who should receive what, it would not have taken many years for his various family members (and others) to fight in court over what he really wanted and what was fair. Of course, this is Jerry Garcia we're talking about. It's hard to imagine him regularly sitting down in conference rooms with attorneys, planning and revising his living trust. But we're sure his widow wished he had.

Chapter Twenty-Two

Everyone knows what an executor or trustee is supposed to do, right? Follow the will or trust, manage the assets, distribute the money, and keep all the beneficiaries happy. Doesn't sound so hard. But when does management become mismanagement? When should beneficiaries worry?

The first red flag to watch out for is so basic that one would think that any executor or trustee would do it without thinking... communicate. Let the beneficiaries know what the will and/or trust says, what assets are in the estate or trust, and keep them informed of progress with administering the assets.

What is Mismanagement?

There is no precise definition of "mismanagement" other than it occurs when a fiduciary, like an executor or trustee, doesn't do his or her job properly. This is an issue of negligence, or unintentional wrongdoing, rather than stealing or self-dealing. These are discussed later.

Doesn't that make sense? How many problems in life happen because people don't talk or share information like they should? The same thing happens when dealing with the affairs of someone who died.

In fact, for both wills and trusts, beneficiaries are entitled by law (at least in the large majority of states) to receive copies of the entire will and those parts of the trust that pertain to them. After that, they are also entitled to receive what is usually referred to as the "inventory."

What do you mean by Inventory?

An inventory is a listing of the assets in an estate or trust. Executors and trustees are generally required to prepare this list in writing and mail it to the heirs to notify them about what is in the estate or trust.

While each state (and sometimes each county) has varying requirements for exactly what level of detail should be in an inventory, the basic rule is that executors and administrators must reasonably inform the beneficiaries of what type of assets there are and what the approximate values are. Not too hard so far... every heir wants to know how big the pie is, so they can figure out how much their piece of the pie will be worth.

Ready for the complicated parts? Let's get to the harder questions. When is the inventory due? How long does a beneficiary have to wait before justifiably complaining when they haven't received an inventory?

Each state has its own time limit. Generally speaking, the limits vary between two to four months or so, from the time that the person officially accepted his or her position as estate executor or trustee. The clock generally does not start ticking from the date of death.

And what about after the inventory is sent? What if you think it is incomplete or something is missing? Then what?

The first step is to ask. Maybe there is a good explanation for something you think is missing. Maybe the executor or trustee forgot or didn't know about something that you knew about, and a quick conversation could have cleared up the confusion.

It is possible that the executor or trustee intentionally excluded the item. Perhaps they didn't include it because the account was closed before the date of death. Or, maybe it was a joint account and wasn't supposed to be included.

On the other hand, maybe it was a joint account that was an account of convenience. (Remember those from Chapter 18?) In that case, you may need to fight to get the asset put back where it belongs, in the estate or trust. Depending on whether the executor or trustee decides to cooperate, you may have to hire an attorney and start a court proceeding.

Once you get past the issue of the initial inventory, what level of information should a beneficiary expect next? The general rule of thumb, in most states, is annual reports. More specifically, these are often called "accountings."

What level of information is included in an accounting? The simplest answer is enough information to fairly inform the beneficiaries of what has been done with the estate or trust property during the time period in question. Many states have forms available that allow the information to be summarized succinctly, with a starting balance, a listing of everything that came in during the last year, as well as everything that was spent or lost, and then a concluding list of what is left. The level of formality required does vary between the states.

Again, it's mostly a matter of common sense. Executors and trustees have a fiduciary obligation, remember? Part of that means they have to, by law, explain what they do with the assets; that's the reason the law requires accountings. The heirs are entitled to see where every dollar went so they can make sure they get their full piece of the pie.

What are Accountings?

An "accounting" is a report prepared by executors and trustees (usually with the help of their attorneys) to "account for" or explain what has happened with the assets of the estate or trust in the past year (or other time period). Some states may use different names for this report. The format can vary, from an official court form to a letter or email. The important part is open communication.

And then there's the big question of mismanagement... what happens when you do get an accounting and it gives you a reason to be concerned? Perhaps there is money missing. Or maybe not enough has been done in the last year... real estate left to sit without being listed for sale, for example. Sometimes there are stocks, mutual funds or other investments that were left in the stock market too long and the stock market tanked, costing the estate or trust hundreds of thousands of dollars.

These events do happen, and a proper accounting should reveal them all. Real estate usually should be sold, not left to sit while the estate or trust pays taxes and insurance (unless there's a good reason). Sometimes family members buy the house, other times it is put on the market, but executors and trustees cannot permit the real estate — often an estate or trust's biggest asset — to linger in most cases.

They also can't ignore stocks and other investments. If the will or trust says to distribute the money promptly, those types of assets should be sold quickly. Why take the risk of a market crash? On the other hand, if the estate plan calls for payments over a longer period of time, the money should be invested with the help of a good financial planner. You can't earn interest on money if it sits around as a pile of cash.

But the most common sign of mismanagement is failing to properly share information, through a formal accounting or otherwise. When executors and trustees don't disclose what they are doing, it causes everyone else to suspect them of wrongdoing. Secrecy is usually the biggest cause of a family feud involving claims of mismanagement.

Didn't your mother tell you never to keep secrets? It is amazing how many executors and trustees forget this rule.

the TRUE STORY
of ROSA PARKS!

Rosa Parks is one of the most famous figures of the civil rights movement. She died on October 25, 2005 at the age of 92. Her 1998 will left everything to the Rosa and Raymond Parks Institute for Self Development in Detroit (a nonprofit organization to educate young people). She named her longtime friend and caregiver, Elaine Steele and a lawyer based in Detroit as her estate executors. In 2003, she amended her will replacing the lawyer with a retired Detroit judge.

Her 13 nieces and nephews were not pleased. Led by nephew William McCauley, they challenged the will, contending Parks signed it while incompetent due to dementia. They also alleged Steele exercised undue influence. McCauley said that the will read like "she didn't care about her family, and that couldn't be further from the truth."

In addition to the challenge to the will itself, the family also claimed Steele and the retired judge violated their fiduciary duties by mismanaging the estate. They felt Steele, who operated the institute and had control of Parks' condominium and her numerous historical possessions located inside, was negligent. For example, they said Steele lost medals and let honorary degrees suffer damage from mold and water. The family also claimed she entered into a secret pact with a celebrity marketing company to profit from Parks' name and image in a commercialized way. They felt Parks never would have condoned it.

They were particularly upset by a $5 billion lawsuit filed on Parks' behalf (when she was still alive but incompetent) against the musical group OutKast for allegedly defaming her through a rap song bearing her name. The family also said Steele withheld financial records.

The probate judge was apparently troubled by the actions of Steele and others. Previously, Steele had voluntarily stepped aside as co-executor, in favor of McCauley, in hopes of appeasing the family. But Steele still ran the institute and controlled Parks' name and likeness. The judge ruled that both co-executors were to be replaced with two independent attorneys he selected.

He then ordered Steele and the institute to refrain from any further secret agreements to profit on Parks' name. This court order almost shut down the Parks Institute, which relied on the funding from the marketing contract to operate. The judge ruled that Steele had to turn over any further profits earned to the new executors.

Those were only the first rulings. The court still had to address whether the will itself was even valid. A jury trial was scheduled in February 2007. An attorney for the relatives predicted it was "going to be a very ugly trial." The trial had much at stake — Parks' estate was estimated to be worth "in the high seven figures."

Steele and the family settled on the eve of trial. While the settlement terms were kept confidential, the Detroit Free Press reported in a March 14, 2007 article that a portion of proceeds from Parks' likeness would be used for her heirs to attend college, the family had the right to represent Parks in dedications of memorials, schools and parks, and an outside company would help oversee the Institute. Additionally, the probate judge ordered many of Parks' possessions to be sold through an auction. The Institute and family members split the money from the auction.

One friend of Steele complained that the settlement left Steele without compensation. However, one of Steele's attorneys said she had been losing sleep over the allegations of undue influence and mismanagement against her. The settlement gave her peace of mind and vindication, she believed, against the allegations that she ever misled or improperly influenced her dear friend.

Yet, like many estates where mismanagement allegations are prominent, the settlement did not resolve all of the fighting. More than two years after the settlement, the court still had to sort through dozens of petitions, objections and other filings. The judge had to rule about the payment of legal and fiduciary fees, whether funds were properly accounted for, and whether marketing agreements were proper. The case continued to be so hotly contested — even after the big settlement — that some parties filed appeals. There is no light at the end of the tunnel as to when the case will finally be resolved.

One can only wonder how Rosa Parks would feel about all of these legal battles. A woman famous for fighting for her values and a seat on a bus... with a legacy tarnished by feuding heirs and administrators.

Are you worried about mismanagement?

Avoid a family fight!

Mismanagement comes in many shapes and sizes. While few estates have as much at stake as Rosa Parks, it doesn't make the proper management of estates and trusts any less important to concerned family members. All trustees and executors must treat their positions with the utmost seriousness and care. While there was likely nothing Steele could have done to avoid the battle altogether, she didn't help her cause by misplacing valuable medals and allowing historic documents to suffer mold and water damage. Given the hotly contested nature of the estate, she never should have entered into a marketing agreement for Rosa Parks' name and likeness without reaching a consensus with the family or seeking court permission. Probate judges will almost always come down hard on fiduciaries if they believe valuable property was damaged or wasted, or if there were secret agreements without proper approval.

Indeed, if Steele had been more transparent in her management, perhaps the family would have been satisfied and the conflict could have been reduced, or even avoided. When a fiduciary has nothing to hide, open communication is usually the best policy.

I guess it's too much to ask for a little loyalty

Chapter Twenty-Three

When it's time for Mom and Dad to create their will or trust, who is the first person they think of when deciding to fill the important role of executor or trustee? Usually it's a son or daughter whom they trust the most to administer their affairs. Of course, this same person is often close to Mom and Dad, which of course means that he or she will also be a beneficiary.

This poses an interesting dilemma that most people don't stop and think about — what does a trustee do when he or she wears two hats — the "administrator" hat and the "beneficiary" hat? These two hats often don't fit comfortably on the same head.

Trustees and estate executors must observe the highest duty of loyalty and good faith.

On the other hand, as beneficiaries, they want to get as much money into their own pockets as possible. Can this pose a conflict? You bet. Sometimes the conflict surfaces in unexpected ways.

The first and most basic is the "fiduciary fee." Both trustees and estate executors are entitled to take a reasonable fee for the

The Duty of Loyalty and Good Faith

This legal duty is another requirement for all executors and trustees. It means they must manage the property for the benefit of all the trust and estate beneficiaries, not for their own interests. They have to be fair to all of the heirs, even when they are tempted to be more than fair to themselves.

services they perform. Usually, this means a fair hourly rate for each hour spent doing trust or estate work.

But what rate is fair? And how does one make sure that the hours for which the fee is paid were actually spent? And what about corporate trustees and administrators? Banks and other financial institutions filling this position usually pay themselves a percentage of the assets in the trust or estate as a fee. Can a family member do the same thing?

Generally, individual trustees and administrators (meaning anyone other than a bank or financial institution) should stick to an hourly rate, unless local practice in the particular state allows for a percentage-based fee. How do you know the local practice? Ask a local probate attorney, of course. He or she can help tell you a normal rate for this type of work. And it can vary depending on the sophistication of the person doing the work and the amount of work needed to be done. If it's selling a house and nothing else, the hourly fee may be lower. If the work involves managing complicated investments by a family member who also happens to be a financial planner, a much higher fee would be appropriate.

And if the work can be done by an outsider at a more reasonable rate, then let someone else do it. Trustees shouldn't pay themselves $75 per hour for cleaning out a house if the same job could be done by a cleaning company at $15 per hour.

Does this mean that every trustee and executor takes a fee? No. In many families, people don't think it would be fair to do so. Every family is different, and every situation is too. Families should talk about the issue and come up with a fair consensus. If they can't do so, then the rule of thumb is that the trustee or executor is entitled to a reasonable hourly fee, if properly documented with a log.

What other conflict situations arise? Personal property is a big one. Often, there is an item or two that everyone would like to have (or sometimes thirty such items!). Trustees and estate administrators usually have the discretion to decide how to divide personal property as long as they do so in a fair and equitable manner.

So, does the trustee get to keep Mom's wedding ring and give different property to the other beneficiaries? Maybe — but not if everyone really wants the ring more than anything else. If the trustee simply decides, "I'm the trustee, I make the decision so I'll keep the ring," the trustee just confused his "administrator" hat with his "beneficiary" hat.

So what to do with personal property when the family disagrees over who gets what? Here are a few options if simple conversation fails:

1.Round robin — draw numbers from a hat and let everyone take turns;

2.Auction — everyone makes a list of what they want; any items that two or more people want should go up for bid; the highest bidder gets the item and pays for it to the trust/estate;

3.Divide the pot — trustee makes equal piles for each person, and then randomly draws straws or flips a coin to assign each pile to a person;

4.Mediator/arbitrator — there are many attorneys and other professionals who will serve as mediator or arbitrator and help divide personal properly (an expensive option for dealing with personal property, but sometimes the best choice in hotly contested situations); and

5.If all else fails — go to court. Let the probate judge decide; that's what he or she gets paid to do.

And what does a trustee do with the inevitable claims of "Mom gave it to me" or "Everyone knows Dad wanted me to have it?"

First, read Chapter Twenty. If that doesn't help, use option five — going to court (we'll cover that in the next chapter).

Another common area of conflict is real estate. It's no wonder that the family home can create drama. Often, the home has sentimental value so some of the heirs may want it to stay in the family. Other times, it's purely about the money. In the majority of estates, the home is the most valuable asset. So, when the house is in the trust or estate, and three children all inherit equal shares, what do you do with it?

Many times, one person is already living there. Other times, no one really wants it, but the real estate market may stink so it's hard to sell.

These difficult questions fall squarely in the lap of the trustee or executor. But, he or she does not get to decide unilaterally to buy the house and exclude the others. Similarly, he or she cannot decide to live in the house for free while slowly administering the estate or trust. Anyone living in a house after the date of death should pay rent... at least enough to pay the taxes, utilities, and insurance.

From there, the administrator has to follow the duty to receive maximum value for the real estate, unless everyone agrees to let someone have the house for less than fair market value for sentimental reasons. This usually means the executor should list the house for sale on the market, or at the very least, obtain an appraisal (that means by an official appraiser — not just a realtor) to set a sales price if sold to a family member or friend.

In estate situations, the executor usually will be required to obtain court approval for any sale. This means he or she should sign the purchase agreement "subject to court approval" and then file the appropriate paperwork with the probate court to have the sale approved before closing occurs on the house.

Then all estate beneficiaries will get written notice of the court hearing and have a chance to come to court and object if they feel the price is not fair. Local procedures may vary by state, and sometimes even by county, so check with a knowledgeable probate attorney and/or the local probate court to be sure.

In trust situations, probate court approval is usually not required. However, if the trustee is also the one buying the house — again the beneficiary hat and administrator hat get jumbled. Obviously, as trustee, the price should be higher, but as purchaser, the trustee will want a lower price. So how do you know the price is fair? The best way is to obtain an appraisal in writing and buy it for that amount (although sometimes it may be fair to reduce what would normally be paid to a realtor if the house had been placed on the open market).

In every aspect of managing an estate or trust, the person in charge must always observe the strictest duty of loyalty and impartiality. In questions of real estate sales, personal property distribution, and fees, what this duty requires isn't always clear cut. But sometimes, executors and trustees act in such a way that there is no question they have breached their fiduciary duty.

And what usually happens then? That's right, an expensive court battle. And, unlike the old westerns where the good guys wore the white hats while the bad guys wore black, it's not always easy to tell the good guys from the bad. (What happened to the mandatory hat policy for good guys and bad guys?)

the TRUE STORY
of DORIS DUKE!

Once known as "the Richest Girl in the World," Doris Duke was heiress to a tobacco fortune. She died at age 80 on October 28, 1993, with an estate estimated to be worth at least 1.3 billion dollars. That's a lot of smokes!

Duke left the bulk of her wealth to charity, to be managed by a charitable foundation established through her will and trust. Reportedly, it was ranked during the mid 1990s as one of the 12 richest foundations in the whole world.

Of course, one would assume that Duke selected a range of the brightest, most charitable and exceedingly well credentialed people to oversee this extensive foundation. Nope. Duke named her butler, Bernard Lafferty, as the lead executor and trustee. She rewarded him with $500,000 annual payments, plus several million dollars more, to compensate him for his services as executor. Routinely described as barely literate, alcoholic, and a lavish free-spender, Lafferty soon faced several different legal challenges.

The attacks included more than one hundred separate allegations — from every angle imaginable. Claimants challenged that the will dated April 5, 1993 was invalid because Duke was incompetent. She had been hospitalized from malnutrition and dehydration when she signed it. Some people alleged Lafferty was guilty of undue influence, improper spending, commingling of assets, waste and faulty management. The allegations didn't stop there. They also made claims against him of kidnapping, intentional drug overdose, and yes, even the M word... murder!

While the more sensational allegations were never proven, the probate judge in New York who heard the case was very troubled by Lafferty's lifestyle and spending habits. He slept in Duke's personal bedroom. He drove her cars, flew in her private jet, and treated her vast assets like his own. Lafferty paid himself a yearly salary of $100,000, in addition to the other money he received, and borrowed more than $800,000 from the estate. He belligerently mixed up his personal assets with estate property, used Duke's credit cards, drank heavily (for which he was repeatedly hospitalized) and took antidepressant medications, sleeping pills and anti-psychotic drugs. The Judge removed Lafferty without even holding a trial.

Lafferty appealed. His attorneys argued that the judge was required to conduct a trial or similar hearing, and that she made the decision based on hearsay. They denied many of the allegations and argued that Lafferty's personal lifestyle should not be considered because Duke's estate had not suffered harm by his actions. They pointed out that Lafferty's relationship with Duke was more like a son than a butler, and he helped her manage her business affairs in life. She chose him and she knew of his lifestyle. Duke's choice had to be respected, the lawyers argued.

Two years after Duke's death, the appellate court ruled, three judges to two, that the probate judge's ruling should stand. They found that while the procedure used by the probate judge was unorthodox, there was enough evidence of wrongdoing to support the decision. Lafferty appealed again.

This time he prevailed. New York's highest court ruled that the probate judge erred by removing him without a trial and Lafferty won his position back. But the fighting had become so expensive and time consuming for the estate that those involved decided to settle.

In the spring of 1996, Lafferty agreed to step down to end the litigation, but he was permitted to keep his fees for life, including the $4.5 million payment and $500,000 per year. In Lafferty's place, the agreement created a board of qualified trustees to manage the charitable foundation.

What was the cost to all this fighting? Seventeen different law firms submitted bills totaling more than $15 million. It took six more years of court hearings and appeals before the courts finally resolved how much of these attorney bills should be paid. In the end, the estate paid almost $10 million in legal fees, not to mention costing many years of lost time during which Duke's chosen charities had to wait to receive any money.

Are you sure the person you've chosen to administer your estate or trust will be able to resist temptation?

Avoid a family fight!

If Doris Duke's butler had been more careful managing the estate after Duke died, the legal fighting would have been reduced and perhaps eliminated. He could have enjoyed a lavish lifestyle and still managed Duke's property fairly. He certainly did not need to use credit cards, the private jet, and even Duke's personal bedroom for his own benefit. Of course, had Duke made a more prudent choice of executor and trustee — especially given her vast wealth — the fighting would have been largely avoided. Duke could have given Lafferty a vote in the manage-ment without giving him total control. Sadly, she invited the fight and the $10 million spent in legal fees by her questionable choice. Yet her choice serves as a lesson to others to be careful in selecting a trustee or executor. Not many people can afford to waste $10 million.

One word of caution... unless you have a vast estate or trust which warrants a board of administrators, be wary of appointing two people to serve as co-executors or co-trustees. As often as not, this leads to conflict because the two may not agree, which may deadlock the adminis-tration.

Hey — he's stealing!

Chapter Twenty-Four

"I don't really trust my brother, the administrator, but he wouldn't actually steal, would he?"

This question runs through the mind of far too many beneficiaries and others concerned about how someone is managing property for an estate or trust. You would think that something as obvious as stealing is easy to spot and easier to remedy, right? Not always.

Certainly there are many cases of outright theft. Many trustees and administrators think that the legal authority to act is really a license to steal. People who are desperate for money often cannot resist the lure of an unguarded pot of gold. Trustees are especially tempted because they generally do not have to worry about court proceedings. They hope their actions will escape unnoticed when no one is guarding the cookie jar.

So they steal. They take. They "borrow." Sometimes they even convince themselves that they have the best of intentions. "I'll pay it back," they think, "before anyone notices the money is gone." Or perhaps they view it as a simple gift... just a little, compared to how much is in the trust. "After all, I'm doing all the work, aren't I entitled to it?"

It's easy to make a "loan" or a "gift" to yourself from the trust or estate if no one is looking over your shoulder. That's why any heir with legitimate concerns should not be afraid to ask for information about what is happening with the trust or estate's assets. If the information suggests that theft may be occurring, that's when it's time to get an attorney (if you don't have one already) and proceed to court. If there is theft or other types of wrongdoing, you can ask the court to remove the person from his or her position of authority, return the missing money or property, and even "surcharge" the wrongdoer.

What do you mean by surcharge?

A "surcharge" is a legal order from a court that a person has to pay money back to the estate or trust when it was wrongly taken, or when money or property was lost through mismanagement or other wrongdoing. In other words, they have to put the cookies back! Sometimes, the person ordered to repay money also has to pay interest, attorney fees and other costs along with it. Different states may use different words for this concept.

The last thing beneficiaries who suspect theft want to do is sit back and do nothing. The sooner they start legal proceedings to recover money, the better their chances are at recovering some or all of what was taken. People who take money usually spend it, and once they get away with it, they often take more and more. The best defense is acting early before too many cats are let loose from the bag.

Think that calling the police or prosecutor will take care of the problem? Think again. Most police and prosecution departments are understaffed and do not have enough resources to pursue these cases, unless the theft is really obvious. But isn't that what cops are for? The problem is that cases like this are often very document-intensive and involve grey areas of whether something was done with criminal intent or not. It is usually up to the people involved to hire attorneys and file proceedings in court to right the wrongs of fiduciary theft.

What if you suspect stealing or similar wrongdoing but can't prove it because the people in charge won't share information? When you ask for information that you're legally entitled to receive and they won't give it to you, they may be trying to hide something. That's often a sign that you have to be more assertive to protect your rights.

In other words, ask to see what's in the cookie jar. If they won't let you see what's there, it may be time to worry.

the TRUE STORY
of THE TRUSTEE WHO COULDN'T BE TRUSTED!

Violet was 86 years old, living in California, when she asked her great niece, Julie, for help. Violet's only son was a substance-abuser and was not trustworthy. Violet owned a wealthy estate of more than $2.5 million. Violet had created a trust to manage the money and picked Julie as the successor trustee. After Violet's doctor wrote a report finding her to be incompetent, Julie took over the role of trustee and moved Violet to Michigan to live with her.

She also took control of the trust's property and sold Violet's home in California. Julie earned a modest living operating a daycare from her home. But Violet, who was suffering from dementia and Alzheimer's disease, needed a great deal of help.

So Julie hired a loyal employee from her daycare business, which Julie then closed, and paid the employee $150 per day to provide around-the-clock care for Violet. For the amount of help that was needed, this sum seemed appropriate.

But Julie felt like she was entitled to something too. So what did she do? She paid herself $300 per day. Julie felt the fee was fair, even though it was twice the amount she paid the person who provided most of the care.

But that was not all. Julie also made "gifts" to herself, her husband and each of her two young daughters in the amount of $12,000, each, per year. She took another monthly fee as compensation for the time she spent writing checks for Violet.

And wait, there's more. Julie decided that Violet deserved a better home. She and her husband bought one — for $480,000. Julie "borrowed" $240,000 from Violet's trust for a down payment, and took out a mortgage for the rest. Since money from the trust was used to buy the house, do you think Julie bought it for the trust? No! She put the house in her name, not Violet or Violet's trust.

Julie later said that she intended to repay this $240,000, as soon as her other house was sold... but she waited to try to sell it. In the meantime, Julie took out a second mortgage on the new house that had been paid for through Violet's trust. Julie used some of the money to buy herself lakefront property so she and her husband could someday build their dream house. She also lent $150,000 to her brother to help him save his house from foreclosure. That sure was nice of her, wasn't it? The problem was that it wasn't her money... that money came from Violet's trust.

When Violet's son passed away, her grandson, Antonio, became very concerned. He was the only beneficiary of Violet's trust, after Violet herself. Antonio hired co-author Andrew, who sent letters to Julie asking her to account for the trust funds and explain what she had been doing with the money. When she didn't provide an accounting, Andrew filed legal proceedings in probate court. The judge ordered Julie to explain what she'd done with the trust money.

After several delays, Julie still hadn't turned over the information. Andrew kept pushing the matter in court until finally Julie's lawyer provided the accounting. Then the real story came out about the $240,000 "loan," the $450 daily fee, the repeated "gifts" and many other questionable uses of trust funds. In total, Julie had gifted away or taken almost $800,000 from the trust in about nine months. The judge was not pleased. He removed Julie and appointed another trustee to manage the trust while the investigation continued into Julie's actions.

Ultimately, Antonio and the trustee agreed to settle the matter when Julie agreed to return the lakefront property to the trust, and Julie's brother came forward to repay the money he had borrowed. But Julie had no other money — everything else had been spent — and the trust could not be made whole. It made no sense to spend more legal fees pursuing Julie when she simply didn't have the money to repay it.

But because Andrew and his client Antonio had taken the matter to court, they were able to save most of the money left in the trust. Had they not done so, they felt quite certain all of it would have been gone.

Do you suspect that a trustee or executor is stealing?

Avoid a family fight!

If you are a beneficiary and have real concerns over how a trustee or other fiduciary is spending the money, do not wait to exercise your legal rights. Talk to an attorney and request a full accounting. If you don't get one, or if the one you get does not answer your questions, do not be afraid to go to court to protect yourself. Trustees and others in charge of someone else's money who are acting properly should have nothing to hide. Look closely for signs of self-dealing, such as gifts or loans, and ask for a new trustee if the old one is not properly fulfilling his or her fiduciary obligations, including refusing to properly share information. Then go to court to make any executor or trustee who stole money pay it back... hopefully before managing to spend it all.

Chapter Twenty-Five

As the stories about Doris Duke and the Trustee Who Couldn't Be Trusted demonstrate, the choice of an executor and trustee is a very important one. You don't want to turn the keys to your family's financial legacy over to someone who may spark a family fight.

Through the years, we've met with countless clients who have had trouble picking a trustee or executor. Sometimes, they've been parents who simply don't want to hurt their children's feelings. Instead of picking the child with the best background to serve, parents may pick the oldest child, the child who lives closest to them, or the child they see most often. And in second-marriage situations, the decision can become even more challenging. Often, there is a great deal of distrust (and even dislike) between the children from the first marriage and the spouse from the second (or in some case, the third, or fourth). Many people in this situation will automatically name the spouse without thinking through how this affects their children.

Be careful not to make a rush decision! Think the options through. Name the person that is best suited to manage your assets and meet the high standards required by law. You need someone reliable, trustworthy, and who has time to do the job. You certainly don't want someone who is already too busy, maybe because they are raising three young children, working overtime or addressing medical problems of their own. But, most importantly, ask yourself this question: Who do you most trust to carry out your wishes and be fair to the heirs and beneficiaries?

Above all, if you can't decide, don't fall into the trap of simply naming everyone possible to act together as your trustees and executors. This is a recipe for disaster! Even the best families may have difficulty administering an estate or trust under these circumstances. There could be geographic issues, such as when the co-trustees live in different parts of the country. Or worse... naming two people who don't get along and expecting them to work together. Many parents think that two children who argue (or don't even talk to each other) will be forced to cooperate if they are both named. Others naively think that, even when the relationship is rocky, the children will get along splendidly when it matters most. Yeah right!

Have you ever had two or more small children? Do you recall what happened when you looked away a moment too long? Remember all the bickering and fighting? Unfortunately, adults can be just as juvenile. Often families change once someone dies and money is on the table. Family members who seem trustworthy can suddenly reveal their latent greedy side. We hear it too often... "I never thought in a million years that this would happen to my family" or "I'm not worried about my children fighting over my money when I'm gone." Believe us, this happens more often than you would expect.

Choosing multiple administrators usually causes more problems than it solves. If you do feel the need to name more than one executor or trustee, build in a couple safeguards. (1.) appoint an odd number of people so deadlocks can be broken by majority rules vote and (2.) if you do have an even number, appoint someone else to act as a tie-breaker to resolve deadlocks. If you do feel the need to name more than one executor or trustee, another option is to use an arbitration or mediation clause. These clauses require conflicts to be decided outside of court, with the goal of saving legal fees (and headaches). Sometimes they help shrink family fights, but other times, they don't help. Ask your estate planning attorney about how these clauses work and whether they may help if you are considering choosing two executors or trustees. Regardless of which approach you choose, it's important that your trustees and executors can resolve a deadlock without having to go to court.

Finally, unless you have an especially valuable or tricky estate or trust, think twice before naming a bank or other corporate fiduciary to serve as administrator or trustee. These entities are expensive, usually charge a percentage of the assets as a fee, and are run by people who won't necessarily care for each family members' concerns like a loved one would. Plus, corporate trustees tend to have a high turnover rate so your beneficiaries may have to work with several different people. But if a family member or another individual isn't appropriate — and when the estate or trust is large enough to justify the costs — then naming a bank or corporation as trustee can be a good choice. Choose wisely though... and make sure to do your homework before selecting a bank or other company to fill this important role.

So what if you suspect that no matter who you name, someone else will be upset and cause trouble? There is no easy answer that applies to every family. Each

What is an arbitration or mediation clause?

As you've seen there are many types of clauses, but these can potentially save your heirs a ton in legal fees. Arbitration clauses require disputes to be decided by a neutral decision-maker (such as an attorney or retired judge) without going to court. Mediation clauses direct people to work with an expert mediator to try to reach a voluntary settlement. Arbitration is binding; mediation is not (unless a resolution is reached). With either option, legal fees are usually a lot less than court proceedings. But they don't always help save money. It depends on the circumstances of each individual case.

person creating a will or trust has to think through the problem and make the decision that works best for their family.

If family friction already exists, you must expect the friction to get much worse when you're gone. Plan ahead and carefully consider who you should select, so a small problem doesn't explode into a larger one. Even if your family only has the potential for disagreements, such as second-marriages or sibling rivalries, make a safe and well-reasoned choice. That's exactly what one of the most famous politicians of recent memory did.

the TRUE CASE STORY
of SENATOR TED KENNEDY!

The will of Senator Edward "Ted" Kennedy was filed with a Massachusetts probate court in late September 2009. It provided a peek behind the curtain of the famed Kennedy family. Ted Kennedy died on August 25, 2009 from brain cancer at the age of 77. He was survived by his wife of 17 years, Victoria, his three children, and two step-children.

Kennedy's will reveals that he did important estate planning that most adults in this country would benefit from... he created a living trust, The Edward M. Kennedy 2006 Trust. His pour-over will directed that all of his assets pass into this trust. The will says that Kennedy's trust provided for his wife, three children, other relatives and for payments of his debts and taxes. So far, so good. But there was no mention of his wife's two children, Kennedy's step-children.

It gets more interesting when you find out who Kennedy hand-picked to serve as executor of his estate and trustee of his trust. Ted Kennedy's family is a classic second-marriage situation. How could Ted Kennedy avoid hard feelings from either his wife or his three children? He had to select a person he felt would be best suited to fairly administer his financial affairs and ensure that all of his beneficiaries were treated fairly. But this person wasn't his wife or any of his children. Hmm... interesting.

It's not like his wife, Victoria, wasn't bright or capable. At 22 years younger than Kennedy, she had youth on her side. Plus, she was a practicing lawyer until 1997.

According to a June 7, 2008 feature article in The Washington Post, Kennedy's friend, Senator Chris Dodd, described her as "a very strong woman" who was "100 percent in control of her husband's care." She was also described as being Kennedy's "principal handler, closest political adviser and now his primary caregiver, juggling his large extended family and his political network, and managing his complicated medical treatment as he battles a potentially deadly cancer."

This was not a meek widow who lacked the skills or expertise to manage Kennedy's estate or trust. Yet he didn't appoint her.

Instead, Kennedy named Paul G. Kirk, Jr. This former chairman of the Democratic National Committee is the very same trusted family friend and confidant who was selected by the Massachusetts governor to temporarily fill Kennedy's Senate seat, until a special election could be held. In fact, Kennedy's family reportedly supported Kirk for the position.

It sounds like a lot to ask of Kirk. Serving these important roles of Senator, executor and trustee is not easy. Too much for one man to handle? The possibility of Kirk having to resign as executor makes Kennedy's back-up choice very important. Yet he still didn't choose his wife. Instead, Kennedy selected one of his children, Edward, Jr.

Why is the choice of executor and trustee such a big deal? According to published reports, Kennedy's publicly-traded assets were listed in a 2008 federal financial disclosure report to be between $15 million and $72.6 million. And that's only a fraction of his total assets, because it doesn't include all of his other investments and property. For example, his home was assessed for tax purposes at almost $10 million.

For those rare estates and trusts which reach the size of the Kennedy family fortune, the jobs of executor and trustee are especially challenging. The person in charge has a great deal of responsibility to be fair to everyone. And this is all the more difficult if there is family friction.

Obviously Kennedy trusted his friend Paul Kirk to handle it. But the person he trusted most after that was his son. Too many second marriage situations erupt into family fights when a husband and father dies. It would be naive to assume that Kennedy didn't think about this when he made his choices.

Did Kennedy know that friction already existed between his wife and his three children? Is that why he made the choices he did? Or had Ted and Victoria Kennedy discussed it and agreed that it would be better if she was left off? Maybe she didn't want the job. Maybe Victoria and Edward, Jr. get along well so there was no concern. But if that was the case, why name Kirk in the first place?

Kennedy and his family obviously trusted Kirk, not only because of his selection in the will, but also because the family backed Kirk to fill the Senate seat. So clearly Kennedy made that choice carefully. And if Kirk isn't too busy for the job, the care Kennedy used in deciding who to pick may have prevented a family fight.

But did Kennedy think through the back-up choice as carefully?

Are you sure the person you've named as executor or trustee will treat everyone fairly and reduce the chances of a family fight?

Avoid a family fight!

Ted Kennedy sure seemed to be concerned about how his choice of executor and trustee would affect the rest of the family. He opted to play it safe with a family friend. This is a great solution for many, when a family fight can be anticipated, but it is a lot to ask of that family friend. It's no fun to be in the middle and have the great responsibility of administering a trust or estate fairly for all heirs and beneficiaries. So make sure to discuss your concerns with the person who you select. You need to know beforehand if he or she is ready for the task at hand.

You can consider naming a trusted attorney, but as we discussed back in Chapter Seven (remember the Michael Jackson story?), this is an option you should only consider if you feel you need to. Certainly do not do it just because your attorney suggests it!

Chapter Twenty-Six

It's not easy to be the one in charge. While many people crave the power, it comes with responsibility, accountability and more often then not, headaches. Remember Jerry Garcia's widow? So stock up on your favorite pain reliever.

This is especially true when someone questions what you are doing. No one who takes on the role of executor or trustee wants to end up in court defending what he or she has done. So how do you do your job the right way and protect yourself?

The first rule is to consult with an experienced trust and estate administration attorney. Does that mean you must spend thousands of dollars on legal fees no matter what? Not necessarily. Of course, if the trust or estate is unusually complicated, is likely to face contested issues or has a large amount of assets to administer, then hiring a good lawyer is a must. But for the more routine, smaller estates and trusts, trustees and executors can possibly get by with a consultation or two. Many attorneys will meet with you and be available to answer questions, for a modest fee, without breaking the bank. That way, those in charge can make sure they follow the steps required in their state.

Plus, the legal fees are costs of the estate and trust... it's not like they have to pay for the attorneys out of their own pocket (except to the extent they are also beneficiaries, in which case they'll pay their fair share when the estate or trust pays the bill).

Next, whether working with an attorney or not, remember the most important rule... communicate. Don't leave the beneficiaries in the dark. After all, when administrators follow the rules, they have nothing to hide, so why not share information? Most dissatisfied heirs become concerned enough to do something about it when they feel like they aren't being kept informed properly. So prepare those accountings at least once a year.

Keep careful records and save receipts. Always keep your personal money separate from estate or trust money. Be willing to let the beneficiaries look through your receipts and back-up documents for the accounting (including check registers) if they ask. Talking to an attorney and communicating openly — it can't be that easy, can it? No, there is more to it than that.

The biggest assets of most estates and trusts are: (1) Real estate, and (2) Stocks, mutual funds or other investments. The key rule to both asset types — protect yourself and the assets. For real estate, that means to make sure the house is properly insured. You need vacant home insurance, not standard homeowners' insurance that won't cover many losses if the house is vacant. Unfortunately, vacant homeowners' insurance usually costs more and covers less than when a home is occupied. Finding a renter usually helps. And always consult with a realtor early in the process; they will help tell you what needs to be done to get the house ready for sale, how much clean-out and updating you should do and what a rough value for the house may be.

But above all, don't procrastinate. Cleaning out a house that may have been lived in decades is not an easy task. Hire help if you need to or want to (remember, nothing requires you to do the manual labor yourself) and get the job done. Houses that sit vacant are harder to sell, cause extra costs that can be avoided (taxes, utilities and insurance while the house sits awaiting a buyer) and are at risk for decline in market values and damage by vandals, burst water pipes and all sorts of other harm. Most people already own their own house. Why worry about taking care of another house too?

For the investments, the key is to act quickly to protect against market decline. The stock market is unpredictable. Be careful. At the very least, consult a financial expert for guidance. You are permitted to hire experts and follow their reasonable advice assuming they are qualified, of course. If you are managing assets, such as stocks and mutual funds, over a period of time, you must also make sure to diversify the investments. Diversification is important, especially for trustees.

What if the person who died didn't have a diverse portfolio? What if they had everything in General Electric and General Motors stock? It doesn't matter. You have a legal duty to follow (which many states call the "prudent investor rule") which means you are required to diversify and treat the investments as a reasonable investor would. Don't keep the stocks in place just because Grandfather liked those stocks — unless, of course, all of the heirs agree (in writing).

Again, it's your rear-end on the line, potentially, if there are losses. Don't take the risk. If you want to invest in a riskier or less-diverse portfolio, only do so with an expert and after notifying all the beneficiaries of your intent. Even better... why not give them the right to express their wishes too? Take their investment objectives into account.

And what do you do if a particularly tough question of administration arises, such as what to do with a house that you want to buy? Ask the court for instructions to protect you and

What is diversification?

All trustees who are required by the trust to keep assets in the trust and only distribute money down the road have to invest the money so it earns interest. When doing so, don't put all your eggs in one basket. "Diversification" means to spread the investments around in different places so there is less risk. But always work with a qualified financial professional to do this the right way.

then follow the instructions the judge gives you. You can do this even for trusts that are otherwise kept out of probate court. Yes, doing this does cost some money, but it's well worth it to protect you. Think of it as buying insurance. If something goes wrong, but the judge said you could do it beforehand, then it's the judge's fault, not yours.

The final area where challenges often arise for administrators is creditor claims. Everyone wants a piece of the inheritance pie. In any estate or trust, the administrator or trustee must address claims of those who feel they are owed money from the person who died. Often, the handling of these claims is routine — paying the final medical bills, funeral expenses, credit cards and utilities, for example. Other times, the claims are muddled, to say the least. Whenever a trustee or executor doubts the validity of a claim, he or she should refuse to pay it and require the person asking for money to bring the matter to court.

But what happens when the person in charge has a personal stake in the matter? There may be emotional involvement, such as when the claimant is a family member of the decedent from a prior marriage. Or sometimes the person asking for money also happens to be a beneficiary... to whom the trustee or executor already owes a fiduciary duty. In these instances, it's not as simple as denying the claim and walking away.

In those cases, the person in charge should not wait for the other party to bring the issue to court, but should bring the claim to the attention of the judge and ask him or her for guidance, or risk being sued later for breach of fiduciary duty.

Communicate, be fair, and when in doubt, ask the other heirs to agree or ask the judge for instructions. Many challenges against estate executors and trustees can be avoided when the person in charge follows these simply directives.

the TRUE STORY
of MARTIN LUTHER KING, JR.!

Perhaps no one has been more aggressive protecting the legacy of a loved one than the family of Martin Luther King, Jr. The estate grew from a small one when King was assassinated on April 4, 1968, with only $30,000 in assets — and not even a will. Over the years the family gained a profit for the estate based on MLK's civil rights legacy. For example, King's manuscripts and other personal items sold for a reported $32 million in 2006.

The King family did all they could to keep the profits in the family. On behalf of the Martin Luther King, Jr. Estate, the nonprofit center bearing his name and the corporation which manages his image and licensing rights, King's family has sent countless "cease and desist" letters and started many lawsuits to make sure that no one profits from King's image, name or speeches without their permission. They even sued CBS for using excerpts from the "I Have a Dream" speech in a video documentary and threatened legal action against street vendors who sold King-Obama "Change" paraphernalia during the Barack Obama inauguration festivities. King's nephew and manager of the King Center said, "If you make a dollar, we should make a dime."

King's son, Dexter King, led most of the action as executor of the King Estate. But his siblings grew concerned that he was too worried about making profits than protecting their father's great legacy. They became frustrated over what they felt was a lack of communication and his refusal to allow them to participate in important decisions affecting the estate.

In July 2008, Dexter's two remaining siblings, Bernice King and Martin Luther King, III, filed a lawsuit against Dexter claiming that he failed to share information with them, refused to turnover financial records and other essential documents, and even "converted substantial funds from the estate's financial account" for his own personal use. The pair's attorney said they felt ignored and were desperate to reopen the lines of communication, even if through a judge.

In the past, the eldest King daughter, Yolanda, kept the family together. But she died of a heart attack, at age 52, in May 2007, one year after their mother, Coretta Scott King, died in January 2006.

The family disagreement was even more costly than most. Dexter King signed a $1.4 million book deal for the estate, which his siblings tried to block by refusing to turn over personal letters between their parents, leading to another lawsuit between them. Then Dexter negotiated yet another deal — this time with Steven Spielberg's DreamWorks Studio for a movie about Martin Luther King's life. Dexter King's siblings were upset because they learned of the deal — after it had been made — by an email. The studio insisted on family unity before the deal could go forward.

More than one year after the family fight lawsuit started, no end was in sight. In fact, Dexter King filed a counter-suit demanding that love letters between MLK and his wife be turned over to him, along with MLK's Nobel Peace Prize. Dexter also asked the judge to dismiss the claims against him, but the judge refused... ordering the case to a full jury trial to determine if Dexter breached his fiduciary duty to his siblings.

Countless millions may be jeopardized if Dexter — the estate executor — and his siblings can't get along. In addition to MLK Jr's financial legacy, the family's name represents an important civil rights legacy. A major film honoring MLK Jr. may never be made if the siblings cannot settle. The stakes are high and the plaintiffs' briefs are long — and yet Martin Luther King Jr.'s name stands for unity, not discord. Once again, check in at TrialandHeirs.com to see how this culture-defining story develops.

Are you an executor or trustee who has done everything you can to protect yourself from legal attacks?

Avoid a family fight!

The King siblings' lawyer who started the lawsuit against executor Dexter King said they didn't know if he had been using the estate and corporate assets for his own personal use, but they presumed he was because he would not share information with them about how he was using them. If this is true, then Dexter King could have avoided costly, time-consuming and emotional litigation simply by communicating openly with his brother and sister. Because he didn't, the estate may lose millions of dollars through the book and movie deals that won't go forward if the family keeps fighting.

This case presents a classic example of the rule that open communication and cooperation can prevent the large majority of fiduciary legal battles. If you become an executor or trustee, share information and your plans openly and honestly. Don't provoke an unnecessary fight. Sometimes sibling rivalries may make this a bitter pill to swallow, but it's almost always wiser to take the high road.

Ideas to Spark Family Discussion

Many estate and trust beneficiaries don't know how to open the lines of communication with family members to avoid a fight. They worry that they'll be perceived as troublemakers. Or perhaps they've already given up on trusting their siblings who have control of the property, and feel asking questions are a waste of time. The easy response to these worries is that you don't know until you try.

If you are content to remain in the dark, then accept it. If not, and a reasonable length of time has passed without proper information, call the person in charge and ask. If that doesn't work, try an email or letter (and keep a copy). Creating a paper trail is always useful if the case does end up in court. Even if it doesn't, putting your questions in writing means there is a better chance they won't be ignored. Avoid talking to others about it until you've communicated with the responsible person first... it can turn catty and gossipy, and that won't help you achieve your interests.

If your first attempts to communicate fail, then enlist other siblings to ask the questions with you. You may not have to go it alone. Or call for a family meeting, and ask your questions then.

Start with the basics: What is in the estate or trust, and what are your plans? Remember, beneficiaries are entitled to receive copies of the will and key portions of the trust, as well as listings of the property and assets owned by the estate and trust. You have the legal right (in most cases) to know what's there. Don't be afraid to ask.

But sometimes that won't work. Sometimes people in charge feel they don't have to answer to anyone. If you face that challenge, and you realize you've reached the point where no answers are forthcoming, then go speak to an experienced attorney. Yuck, right? Don't worry, they've dealt with it before, and they're on your side. The legal fees spent may save much more down the line. Fiduciaries who ignore informal requests for information will seldom ignore an attorney's letter. It's amazing how powerful a well-written lawyer's letter can be in these cases.

And don't hesitate to mention the cases from this Section to your family members as examples of what can happen when there isn't proper communication. No family wants to end up feuding like Jerry Garcia or Martin Luther King's heirs. Work those examples into casual conversation and follow them up with a simple statement like, "Thank God our family isn't like that!" Then start asking your questions. Once you break the ice, you'll probably be surprised at how easy the conversation will flow.

And what is the best way to avoid conflicts about improper trust or estate management? Choose wisely when you name your executor or trustee in your estate plan, and encourage your loved ones to do the same.

Just like Ted Kennedy, if there is a second-marriage family or one where the siblings just don't get along, it makes selecting someone who is likely to minimize fighting rather than increasing it all the more important. Think through the choice very carefully and don't rely on shortcuts like picking the oldest child or the closest relative.

CONCLUSION

Congratulations are in order... You've learned a ton, and now you're on the home stretch!

In Section I we posed the rhetorical question "A WILL IS SIMPLE, RIGHT?" NOT SO FAST. As you now know, a will leads straight to probate court even if it's prepared correctly. Then in Section II we explored the difference between wills and trusts... so you could say "NOW WE'RE GETTING SOMEWHERE. I NEED A TRUST." But moving into Section III, we learned all about will and trust contests and the need to watch our back because PEOPLE ARE CRAZY, RELATIVELY SPEAKING. They can argue about all sorts of things as we learned in Section IV about ASSET DISPUTES — "BUT THEY WANTED ME TO HAVE IT!" And finally, Section V showed us how to tell if the THE EXECUTOR IS SCREWING IT UP and what to do about it.

Before class is dismissed... we have a couple more juicy stories for you, and they'll help us review all that you've learned. Fair warning though! Baseball legend Ted William's story is a bit creepy as his descendants fought over freezing or cremating his body. Which one do you think he really would have wanted? And we've all heard about Anna Nicole Smith... but what led to her infamous tabloid dramas? Was she the poster child for a gold-digger or a legitimate heiress to a fortune? Did she ever get the millions she fought for? Stay seated for this exciting conclusion!

the TRUE STORY
of TED WILLIAMS!

Ted Williams is widely recognized as one of the greatest hitters ever to play the game of baseball. He died in Florida on July 5, 2002 at the age of 83. He was survived by three children, who had two different mothers. Barbara Joyce Ferrell was the eldest; she was twenty years older than her two half-siblings, John Henry Williams and Claudia Williams. Williams cut Ferrell out of his 1996 will "because I provided for her during my life." She was a beneficiary of his trust, however.

Ferrell and her half-siblings were on opposite sides of a very emotional and expensive family feud in probate court. But it was not about whether Ferrell was properly excluded from the will. Instead, they fought over whether their famous father should be cryogenically frozen in case medical science ever developed a way to bring him back to life. The 1996 will spelled out Williams' desire for cremation, with his ashes "sprinkled at sea off the coast of Florida where the water is very deep." Ferrell and some of Williams' longtime friends said he often remarked that he wished to be cremated.

But John Henry and Claudia felt otherwise. Very shortly after their father died, they flew his body to Scottsdale, Arizona and froze it. To support their actions, they produced a grease-stained, handwritten note that they said had been signed by them and their late father in a hospital room. The note, dated November 2, 2000, stated:

> JHW, Claudia, and Dad all agree to be put into bio-stasis after we die. This is what we want, to be able to be together in the future, even if it is only a chance.

Ferrell claimed the note was forged and wasn't legally valid. She and her attorneys fought to have Williams unfrozen and cremated, according to his will. Ferrell believed her half-brother only wanted the body frozen so he could sell samples of the DNA. In August 12, 2003, the Associated Press wrote that a Sports Illustrated reporter claimed to have a taped conversation proving that 182 DNA samples had been taken from Ted Williams' body, eight of which were mysteriously missing.

However, the fight grew too expensive. Ferrell said she and her husband spent $87,000 from their retirement savings to fund the lawsuit and were out of money. They publicly asked for donations to help their case, but their efforts failed. So Ferrell agreed to drop the case in exchange for the immediate release of the trust assets to her and her fellow heirs, rather than waiting as spelled out in the trust. This means Ferrell received $215,000 ten years sooner than she otherwise would have.

Still, Ferrell didn't let the matter rest. (You didn't think because a settlement was reached the family feud was over did you?) She moved from a civil case to a criminal case. Ferrell and her husband asked authorities to prosecute her half-siblings, because they had proof that Claudia Williams wasn't in the room when the note had been signed. Florida state prosecutors said that testing showed Ted Williams' signature was valid and the same ink was used for both his and John Henry's signatures. They felt that Claudia's possible absence from the room didn't give rise to a crime (at least one that could be prosecuted).

Ferrell was deeply disappointed by the lack of prosecution. But she took comfort from her efforts to honor her father's memory by doing all she could to uphold what she believed were his true wishes.

Those of you with weak stomachs may want to skip this paragraph. Because the instructions in the greasy note were followed — not those in the earlier will — Ted Williams' body was decapitated. His head was shaved, drilled with holes and accidentally cracked ten times, on August 12, according to the Associated Press in 2003. The lab stored the remaining body upright in a nine-foot steel tank, filled with liquid nitrogen. The procedure cost $136,000 — undoubtedly much more than the costs of sprinkling his ashes into the sea.

Pretty gruesome, huh? We told you family feuds could get messy!

Are you concerned about fighting with siblings after your parent dies?

Avoid a family fight!

Family feuds in probate court between siblings are common. Sibling (and half-sibling) rivalries tend to involve many emotions that extend cases beyond simple greed. Feelings of favoritism, distrust, jealousy and resentment can simmer under the surface for years and then explode after the death of a parent, causing very messy battles. Yet many of these disputes still come down, in the end, to money. Ferrell was obviously very emotional when battling her half-siblings over the best way to honor their father's wishes. But money caused her to settle. It's not easy to put emotions aside and focus on the business decision of when to fight and when to compromise. But after the emotional damage is done, it's the only way to survive a fight of this magnitude.

Can you imagine?

The Ted Williams case highlights the two common threads of most probate family feuds: they are emotional and often expensive.

His daughter did not want to see his body decapitated and frozen in liquid nitrogen; she wanted his ashes spread over the deep Florida sea as his will dictated. But she couldn't afford to carry on the battle. Clearly the emotions took their toll as well.

And that's why the proper estate planning is so important. If Williams did change his mind, he should have changed his will. An attorney could have met with him in the hospital to make sure that a codicil (amendment) or new will was executed properly and confirmed his intent. A grease-stained note left too much doubt.

You've graduated!

One of the main reasons for writing this book was to teach readers how to protect their own families so they don't end up in legal feuds like this one. Of course, very few families fight over whether to cryogenically freeze a body — but battles over wills, trusts, bank accounts and other assets are far too common. So consider yourselves graduates of Trial & Heirs™ 101! You are now armed with the essential questions and knowledge to set things right in your family.

You owe it to your family (and more importantly yourself!) to put your own wishes in writing through a properly drafted estate plan. Who doesn't want to maintain control over their assets and wishes during their lifetime AND after death? Especially those of us with Type A personalities! With the proper plan and a good estate planning attorney, you can achieve this... assuming you're mentally competent and over the age of 18.

After reading this book, you're officially empowered! You have information that can help you maintain control over your wishes and decrease the chances of family feuds. Remember, the only good legal battle is one that never happens. Let's review:

1. You know why wills are important, and what limitations they have. They are public, must pass through probate court, result in court fees and often costly attorney bills, do not help people until after death, and often are easier to challenge in court than trusts.

2. You've learned about the better estate planning tool... a living trust. You also understand that a trust needs to be funded to work effectively, and that it can help people maintain control through the use of detailed, creative instructions to make sure their money passes exactly as they want. You know to avoid pre-made trust kits and why trusts can't usually help you escape creditors. And don't forget about providing for special needs children, minimizing estate taxes, keeping your affairs private and, of course, reducing the chances of a family fight.

3. You now know how messy will and trust contests can be and why they are to be used with caution, what legal tests apply to them, and what to do if you're in one. Legal challenges can succeed when wills and trusts fail the test of formalities, were signed by someone lacking sufficient mental capacity, or were prepared because of undue influence. But, they're never easy for anyone involved.

4. You understand the pitfalls of using joint tenancy (for bank accounts and real estate in particular) and why taking shortcuts can create more problems than they solve. You've learned not to undermine your own estate planning by using joint ownership, conflicting letters or verbal gifts. And don't forget about the problems life insurance can cause when it's inconsistent with your estate plan.

5. Finally, you know the importance of choosing a good executor and trustee, and not exposing your family and legacy to a fight over mismanagement. You've learned what level of communication to expect and what rights you have as an heir.

We've saved the grandaddy of estate cases to highlight some of these lessons that you've learned.

the TRUE STORY
of ANNA NICOLE SMITH!

It ranks as perhaps the most famous probate litigation case ever —
Marshall v. Marshall (a.k.a. the former centerfold versus the son
of her late 90-year old husband). Anna Nicole Smith, whose real
name was Vickie Lynn Marshall, was a 26-year old topless dancer
and former Playboy Playmate of the Year when she married for
the second time. The happy groom was none other than 89-year
old Texas oil tycoon, J. Howard Marshall, II.

Sadly, the love-filled marriage lasted only 14 months, until the
elder Marshall died in 1995. In that brief time, he showered Smith
with valuable gifts. In total, he gave her more than six and a half
million dollars in property before and during their marriage. Of
course, that's merely a drop in the bucket. Marshall's considerable
fortune was valued at $1.6 billion. Marshall's will and trust left
none of it to Smith.

Instead, he left it all to the younger of his two sons, E. Pierce
Marshall (who was 27 years older than his "step-mother"). Pierce's
brother, J. Howard Marshall III, had been disinherited through
their father's 1992 will and trust. Reportedly, the late Marshall II
wasn't happy that his namesake chose the side opposite of him
during a shareholder dispute, so he chose Pierce as his heir.

So, of course, Anna Nicole Smith and Marshall III both filed
legal challenges. Marshall III claimed his father promised not
to disinherit him, and Smith alleged he promised her one-half
of all he owned. They both said that Pierce Marshall improperly
interfered with Marshall II's attempts to revise his estate plan
before his death.

They did have some evidence on their side. Marshall II granted
Pierce power of attorney just after he married Smith. Pierce used

the legal authority to cancel credit cards for Smith and stop payment on a one million dollar check his father had written for Smith to buy jewelry.

The case was filed in a Texas probate court in 1995. To complicate matters, in order to protect herself against lawsuits from other people, Smith filed for bankruptcy in California in January 1996. Pierce Marshall filed a claim against her in the bankruptcy court based on defamation — claiming that Smith had defamed him when she said publicly that he committed fraud and forgery to prevent her from inheriting. Smith, of course, counterclaimed through the bankruptcy court and alleged he really did those things.

In other words, Marshall v. Marshall went forward in two court systems, in two different states: The Texas state courts and the federal court system (because bankruptcy courts are federal courts) in California.

The California court case was decided first. Smith won a judgment against Pierce Marshall for $475 million (yes... you read that right... $475 million!) much of which consisted of "punitive" damages because the court believed there was significant evidence of fraud and similar wrongdoing by Pierce Marshall. The case then went before another judge in the federal court system in California who reduced the amount to a paltry $88 million.

Both California judges found Pierce Marshall conspired to stop Howard Marshall II from creating a new trust that was to leave half of the appreciation of his assets that occurred during the 14-month marriage to Smith. In other words, while they felt Marshall II wasn't going to leave Smith half of everything, he was going to give her half of the increase in value of his property and investments earned during the marriage.

That is, Marshall II was going to do so, until Pierce Marshall wrongly interfered, according to both federal judges in California. They ruled Pierce backdated, altered and falsified documents, arranged for surveillance of the happy couple, and presented documents to his father under false pretenses. The judges described the evidence against Pierce as "overwhelming."

Because of her victory in California (by the first judge, but before the second judge ruled), Smith withdrew her claim in the Texas probate court. But the case still went to a jury trial, because Marshall III hadn't dropped his claims. The jury then ruled that Pierce Marshall did nothing wrong, and the 1992 will and trust were declared valid. The jury also found that Marshall II never promised Smith half of his estate.

So which ruling would win out? Good question. In fact, that's the big question. Pierce Marshall appealed the California decisions and successfully convinced the Ninth Circuit Court of Appeals to rule that the whole case was a probate matter, so the federal courts had to stay out (for lack of jurisdiction). Smith lost her victory and her $88 million judgment.

Smith challenged the ruling. She asked for an appeal to the United States Supreme Court. Because that Court is the highest in our country, it accepts very few cases — only ones that have real importance to our country's laws. Yet it decided to take this case. And it ruled in favor of Anna Nicole Smith! The federal courts could hear the case, even though questions of this matter are typically related to probate proceedings, which normally only proceed in state courts.

But that decision only marked a victorious battle for Smith, not the whole war. The Supreme Court sent the case back to the Ninth Circuit Court of Appeals to decide other issues. Namely, was it proper for the second California judge to enter judgment for Smith when he did so after the Texas probate case was already decided in favor of Pierce Marshall? Yet another very good question.

In fact, as of today, we don't have an answer to it. Pierce Marshall died shortly after the United States Supreme Court issued its decision. Then Anna Nicole Smith died less than a year after Pierce Marshall passed. And no, the case doesn't end just because the two combatants died. Rather, their estates are continuing the battle. Even after death the two are still battling!

However, the Ninth Circuit put a freeze on the case until Pierce Marshall's estate could be sorted out. Attorneys for Anna Nicole Smith's estate asked the Supreme Court to order the case to be unfrozen (in legal terms, to "lift the stay"). The Supreme Court refused to do so in March 2009.

So, here we are, fourteen years (and counting) after J. Howard Marshall II died. Years of litigation, appeals and fighting lay ahead before his estate can be resolved.

In the meantime, Anna Nicole Smith's estate had plenty of legal fighting of its own. Most importantly, Smith's failure to name a guardian in her will opened the door to a big court feud over who should care for her infant daughter. But that's a story for another day. (Or more specifically, a future book!)

It will be interesting to see if that daughter ever receives any of J. Howard Marshall II's money. And if she does, will she be an adult by the time she receives it?

Be sure to check in with TrialandHeirs.com to find out how this case ends.

How can you use the knowledge you've gained in this book to make sure your wishes are followed?

Avoid a family fight!

The only probate family feuds more emotional than sibling rivalries are second marriage situations, particularly where the new spouse is around the same age (or even much younger) than the adult children from the prior marriage. Anyone in such a family must take the utmost care to address his or her estate planning needs the right way.

This case also demonstrates the importance of working with quality attorneys. If Pierce Marshall's attorneys had handled the case differently, these issues never would have been raised in the bankruptcy court — keeping the case in the Texas probate court system, where he won. Credit Anna Nicole Smith's attorneys for seizing the opportunity to help her case — to the tune of an $88 million judgment.

Never underestimate skillful lawyering! Yes, we realize we may sound a bit like a broken record on this point... but it *is* that important.

Which brings us to our final question... have you selected an attorney to help you set up your estate plan yet? We've put together some suggestions to guide you as you make your decision.

First, remember what you've learned here. The knowledge you've gained will aid you in your own estate planning and give you the basics to help you find the right estate planning attorney... or a probate litigation attorney if you're in a family fight. Either way, you should interview different lawyers and find one you are comfortable with and who specializes in these fields.

In doing so, ask lots of questions and test their knowledge. Remember, it's not the number of grey hairs that an attorney has, but his or her experience in the fields of estate planning or probate litigation that matters. A few good questions to ask either type of attorney are: (1.) What percentage of his or her practice is estate planning or family fights? (2.) How long has he or she practiced law in this specific area? (3.) Has he or she had any bar complaints? (4.) Does he or she have any client or professional testimonials? (5.) Can he or she intelligently discuss the legal concepts that you've learned through this book? (Hint: throw out some of the new terms you've learned to show that you understand the language. It can win respect with a good attorney and help you spot an inexperienced one.)

Compare the answers to these 5 questions among the attorneys you talk to.

And for those messy family fights, we have a few more questions for you to ask potential probate litigation attorneys: (1.) Can he or she tell you about the laws in your state that control joint bank accounts and insurance beneficiary designations? (2.) How do the laws work when they contradict the will or trust? (3.) What exactly do you need to prove in order to establish undue influence in your state? (4.) What criteria is used to determine when someone is found to be mentally incompetent? (5.) What steps does he or she recommend when faced with a trustee or estate executor who isn't doing a good job?

If the attorney you interview can't give you intelligent, concrete answers to these questions, it may be time to move on to someone else.

And remember, a good probate litigation attorney will guide you skillfully through the complexities of probate court and help you right the wrongs you feel duty bound to address. But be wary of those who want to rush you to court to earn a buck.

If you are left with a feeling that they are more interested in your money than you, or if you suspect you know more than they do, then you should probably hire a different attorney. Find an attorney that is capable. Some lawyers will prepare an estate plan or take on a contested probate case like the ones described in this book, without having the experience and expertise to do so. Yes, it's true, some lawyers will take whatever case they can just to get paid! Watch out for such attorneys. You're usually better off going with experience.

Just as you would not go to a podiatrist for heart surgery, make sure that you go to the proper attorney to meet your legal needs. Don't assume that because someone is an attorney, that they specialize in everything! Chances are that a criminal attorney wouldn't do estate planning properly and a bankruptcy lawyer would not have the expertise for a family fight.

Even if you are inclined to work with a particular attorney, it's usually a good idea to meet with more than one attorney to compare. You shop around for the perfect home, car, even a pair of shoes, so make sure that you shop around for the BEST attorney for you. This doesn't mean shopping for the cheapest; rather select the most qualified attorney to meet your needs.

And, yes, working with an experienced estate planning or probate litigation attorney does sometimes cost more. But it will usually be well worth it in the end.

And never be afraid to ask questions of your attorney. Remember, you're empowered with information now! If you do want additional help finding an attorney, you can visit TrialandHeirs.com.

Will proper estate planning avoid a probate fight after death? Not always. But it sure can help. And clearly, the alternative of not doing so is asking for trouble.

Peace of mind.

This is the priceless comfort that you will experience once you put your affairs in order through the proper estate planning.

Control.

When you make sure your wishes will be followed, even after you pass away, you can be certain that the lifetime of savings you worked so hard for will be used precisely how you want.

Justice and fairness.

While it's never easy fighting in court, sometimes it's necessary to protect loved ones, honor the memory of the one who passed, and guard or pursue what's rightfully yours.

Knowledge.

This is what we have gathered for you, providing a unique glimpse behind the scenes of "famous fortune fights!" We hope the examples have helped to demystify the subject of estate planning for you and encouraged you to talk to your loved ones about it.

Now take this KNOWLEDGE and use it as a tool to find PEACE OF MIND, maintain CONTROL, and achieve JUSTICE AND FAIRNESS.